INSIGHT COMPACT GUIDE

COSTA Blanca

Compact Guide: Costa Blanca is the ultimate quick-reference guide to this popular destination. It tells you all you'll need to know about the attractions of Spain's southeast Mediterranean coast, from its fabulous beaches and resorts, to its ancient towns and rolling lands of orange and almond groves.

This is one of 133 Compact Guides, combining the interests and enthusiasms of two of the world's best-known information providers: Insight Guides, whose innovative titles have set the standard for visual travel guides since 1970, and Discovery Channel, the world's premier source of nonfiction television programming.

D0581281

DISCOVERY
CHANNEL

APA PUBLICATIONS

Part of the Langenscheidt Publishing Group

Insight Compact Guide: Costa Blanca

Written by: Robert Möginger
English version by: Paul Fletcher
Photography and cover picture by: Gregory Wrona
Additional photography by: Paul Almasy/Corbis (p105)
Design: Roger Williams
Picture Editor: Hilary Genin
Maps: Polyglott/Maria Randall

Editorial Director: Brian Bell
Managing Editor: Tony Halliday

CONTACTING THE EDITORS: As every effort is made to provide accurate information in this publication, we would appreciate it if readers would call our attention to any errors and omissions by contacting:
Apa Publications, PO Box 7910, London SE1 1WE, England.
Fax: (44 20) 7403 0290
e-mail: insight@apaguide.co.uk

Information has been obtained from sources believed to be reliable, but its accuracy and completeness, and the opinions based thereon, are not guaranteed.

© 2004 APA Publications GmbH & Co. Verlag KG Singapore Branch, Singapore.

First Edition 2002; Updated 2004
Printed in Singapore by Insight Print Services (Pte) Ltd
Original edition © Polyglott-Verlag Dr Bolte KG, Munich

Worldwide distribution enquiries:
APA Publications GmbH & Co. Verlag KG (Singapore Branch)
38 Joo Koon Road, Singapore 628990
Tel: (65) 6865 1600, Fax: (65) 6861 6438

Distributed in the UK & Ireland by:
GeoCenter International Ltd
The Viables Centre, Harrow Way, Basingstoke,
Hampshire RG22 4BJ
Tel: (44 1256) 817 987, Fax: (44 1256) 817 988

Distributed in the United States by:
Langenscheidt Publishers, Inc.
46–35 54th Road, Maspeth, NY 11378
Tel: (1 718) 784 0055, Fax: (1 718) 784 0640

www.insightguides.com

Costa Blanca

Introduction

Places

Culture

Practical Information

▽ **Guadalest (p65)**
The bell tower of La Asunción is a symbol of Alicante province.

◁ **Xàtiva (p73)**
Many splendid medieval buildings can be found in this historic town.

▽ **Peníscola (p 42)**
This is considered the most attractive resort on the Costa del Azahar.

△ **València (p24)**
Side by side with the Gothic splendour of València is this example of late-Baroque architecture, the Palau del Marquès de Dos Aigües, with its playful and highly ornate facade.

▽ **Caravaca de la Cruz (p91)** The town is best known for a miracle-performing cross, kept in the shrine of the 15th-century castle.

△ **Morella (p47)** This is Santa María La Mayor, a beautiful Gothic church, and one of the many fine medieval buildings in Morella.

△ **Benidorm (p65)** Ideal if you like high-rise hotels and round-the-clock entertainment.

▷ **Murcia (p81)** Highlights are the stunning Baroque cathedral and the delicious food.

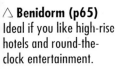

◁ **Teruel (p51)** The Torre El Salvador is one of Teruel's many fine buildings; the town is widely acknowledged to be the pinnacle of Mudéjar architecture.

▷ **Alicante (p54)** Explanada de Espanya is probably the finest promenade on the Spanish Mediterranean.

More than just Sol y Playa

The Mediterranean lifestyle means warmth, vitality, spontaneity and individuality. It is probably best expressed in the colourful images produced by the Catalan painter, Joan Miró, whose famous bright yellow sun symbol has become the logo for the Spanish National Tourist Board.

Yet those who initially come to València or Murcia just for the sandy beaches and the climate will find themselves inescapably drawn by the region's fascinating history. Like fossils in a quarry, traces of many different civilisations lie buried just below the surface, even in the tiniest provincial village: Baroque cathedrals built on the foundations of Moorish mosques, Visigoth settlements on Roman theatres, and beneath them traces of the Carthaginian, Greek or Celto-Iberian era. The Arabic heyday, that period when Muslims, Christians and Jews lived in harmony together and took science and art to the highest level, is very much in evidence.

Opposite: Altea view
Below: the national fruit
Bottom: Calle Major, Cehegín

LOOK BEYOND BENIDORM

Today, even though Spain has a key role to play in modern Europe, the Levant coast retains much of the character that gives it a unique place among the other regions on the Iberian peninsula. The soul of its inhabitants is revealed in the countless fiestas held between Águilas and Vinaròs. Nothing ever happens without good food, strong wine, music and a cacophony of fireworks.

But the Costa Blanca – isn't it associated with the dubious pleasures of mass tourism so typical of the early years of the Spanish holiday boom? All those dreadful high-rise hotel blocks in Benidorm, the all-day breakfast cafés and the beaches where sun-worshippers lie packed together on the sand like sardines in a tin? Yes, they are still there. But, for the past few years, holidaymakers and tour operators have been focusing their attention elsewhere, away from the seaside promenades and the *playas*. Southeast Spain is now confidently marketing itself as a historically mature region with a rich cultural heritage, a varied natural landscape and some fascinating towns well away from the *sol y playa*. The Costa Blanca is no longer a synonym for the whole region; it is just one of many pieces in the mosaic of a region which is well worth exploring.

Below: Sax castle on the 'Castle Road'
Bottom: windsurfing off Parque Regional Calablanque

LOCATION

The southeast of the Iberian peninsula, also known as the Spanish Levant, consists of the region between the Ebro delta in the north and Andalusia in the south. In political terms, this part of Spain belongs to two autonomous regions, València (23,305sq km/9,000sq miles) and Murcia (11,317sq km/4,370sq miles). Strictly speaking, the Costa Blanca comprises the narrow coastal strip from Dénia to La Manga . The tourist industry is largely responsible for inventing the names given to other coastal strips, e.g. Costa del Azahar (Vinaròs to València), Costa de València (València to Dénia) and Costa Cálida (Murcia). València's coastline extends for 485km (300 miles, Murcia's for 176km (109 miles).

LANDSCAPE

Characteristic features of the coast in the northern provinces are wide, sandy beaches, often lined by dunes. The photogenic rocky outcrops jutting out to sea, such as Penyal d'Ifac (near Calp), have become symbols for some holiday resorts.

In the middle of the marshy plain, between the mouths of the rivers Túria and Júcar, lies the freshwater lagoon known as L'Albufera. Salt marshes and flats interrupt the fine-sand beaches to the south of Alicante, while the narrow peninsula of La Manga ('The Sleeve') separates the lagoon of El Mar Menor ('The Smaller Sea') from the open sea. The foothills of the mountain ranges in the hinterland break up the Murcian coast into beautiful bays and rocky peninsulas. Trade, fishing and tourism bring employment to the coastal region,

FRANCE

Madrid

PORTUGAL

València

SPAIN

Mediterranean Sea

MOROCCO   ALGERIA

making it the most densely-populated area and the political and social heartland of the Levant.

The mountains *(sierra)*, some 50 to 100km (30 to 60 miles) away from the coast, are part of two extensive ranges: the Cordillera Ibérica in the northwest and the Cordillera Bética in the southeast. Some peaks exceed 2,000 metres (6,500ft) and may get a covering of snow in the winter.

In the transitional zone beneath the barren plateau *(meseta)* of Castilla-La Mancha and Aragón lie the peripheral provinces of Maestrazgo and northeastern Murcia. The broad and empty *sierra*, with its virtually vegetation-free, sun-baked lunar landscape, has a special appeal to visitors from temperate, north European climes.

The highest peak in Murcia is Pico Revolcadores (2,027m/6,650ft), and in València it is Penyagolosa (1,813m/5,948ft).

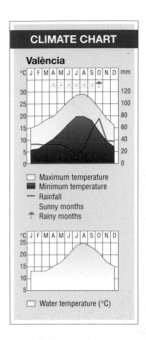

CLIMATE CHART

València

☐ Maximum temperature
■ Minimum temperature
— Rainfall
   Sunny months
🌂 Rainy months

☐ Water temperature (°C)

CLIMATE

The almond and orange trees are already in blossom while much of northern Europe is still immersed in winter gloom. The climate in the Spanish Levant is typically Mediterranean and extremely mild. The warm to hot summer lasts for almost three quarters of the year, at least along the coastal zone. It gets cooler from December to February. August is the hottest month, with

Almond groves at Caravaca de la Cruz, near Mula

temperatures averaging just under 30°C (86°F), while in January temperatures hover around 15°C (59°F). Rainfall is low (about 400mm/16 inches annually), with most of that falling in late autumn and early spring.

After heavy rain, the parched earth is often unable to absorb the water and this leads to flash floods, with water from the mountains rushing along what are known as *ramblas* (dry beds) on their way to the sea. Some parts of Murcia (e.g. the Abanilla lowlands) have a North African, desert-like feel, because there is often no rain from one year to the next.

From July to September, when the mercury can rise to over 40°C (104°F), a heat haze known as the *calina* often hangs over the hinterland; by the beach, however, a cooling breeze usually provides refreshing relief from the fierce sun.

This part of Spain is affected by two persistent wind patterns: the hot dry *poniente* blows down from the Castilian plain, while the *levante* brings in warm, moist air from the southeast.

Below: Fonts de l'Agur
Bottom: farmhouse near Cantavieja

WHEN TO GO

For tourist purposes, July to September and Easter week *(Semana Santa)* are high season. The roads are busy, the beaches crowded and the holiday hotels often full – prices tend to be higher too.

If your visit to Spain is not just for the Mediterranean beaches, then go for the low season (March to June, October to December), when the weather is much more agreeable. Many hotels close for at least part of the winter for renovation work.

NATURE

Man has been shaping the face of the Levant for thousands of years. The trees and bushes that dominate much of Mediterranean Spain have now replaced most of the original vegetation. Olive, almond and citrus trees were planted on the open fields or terracing centuries ago, but now apricot, peach, carob and fig plantations also occupy large swathes of land.

Wine is produced in the interior, e.g. near Requena and Jumilla, while vegetables are grown in the *huertas*. This is the alluvial land close to the coast, which is usually flat and fertile and in some places extends deep inland. Derived from the Latin *hortus* meaning market garden, the *huertas* have traditionally been used for arable farming, with the most fertile land to be found in the València region and in the triangle between Murcia, Alicante and the Mar Menor.

In the southwest of the region towards La Mancha, sunflowers are a common sight in fields, as are the violet flowers of the purple autumn crocus, which in late summer yield the yellow colouring essential for the national dish of paella.

A little room remains amid the cultivated land for chestnut oaks, cork oaks and oleander. But almost everywhere is *matorral*, a tough, drought-resistant shrub amid a scattering of prickly pear cacti and agaves. A few reminders of the once-dense Mediterranean deciduous upland forest survive, e.g. in the Sierra Mariola, or in the north of Murcia, where strawberry trees, broom, palmetto and thyme also thrive.

FAUNA

Spanish fauna is similar to that found in northern and central Europe. Iberian red deer are a fairly

Sea and sand

These are still the Costa Blanca's principal assets. It is not just the 2,500 fishermen between Dénia and Torrevella who depend on the condition of the water, but also the whole of the tourist trade. That is why the authorities very proudly display the 'blue flag' *(bandera azul)*. In 2003, València and Murcia won this prestigious award for 86 beaches and 20 ports, representing 20 percent of blue flags awarded in the country overall.

Critics point out that the blue flag rewards the provision of first-aid posts or the number of rubbish bins just as much as the quality of water. But at the very least the flag is a symbol of good intentions, because wherever it hangs, the sand is cleaned regularly and the water investigated thoroughly for bacteria.

Sunflowers – a common sight in the southwest

frequent sight. The few remaining mountain forests provide habitats for the occasional genet, introduced from north Africa, and other smaller mammals such as weasels and foxes. Geckos and various types of lizards can often be seen lying in wait for passing insects. No one needs to worry about poisonous snakes. The Lataste viper does inhabit this part of the world and has a poisonous bite, but it generally shuns human company.

Many different bird species can be found along the coast. Storks, ducks and flamingos nest in L'Albufera lake near València and the salt marshes of the southern Costa Blanca. By far the best time for bird watching is between March and May, when many migratory birds stop off here to rest. Birds of prey, notably golden eagles, hawks and griffon vultures, can often be seen circling above the barren Maestrazgo plains.

> **Natural parks**
> The best known *parques naturales* within the region are the pine forests of the Sierra de Espuña and the wetlands of L'Albufera. Others include the Peñon d'Ifach near Alicante, Mount Montgó to the south of Dénia, and the Font Roja, one of the last remaining areas of mixed Mediterranean woodland.
> In the mid-1990s, the string of salt lakes down the coast were designated a natural park: Parque Natural de las Salinas, host to grebes, flamingos and a wealth of wading birds. At the Santa Pola saltpans 250 species of bird have been observed.

L'Albufera lagoon

ENVIRONMENTAL CONCERNS

As is apparent from the piles of rubbish left lying around on picnic sites and by bathing areas, the Spanish people's concern for the environment is outweighed by the importance of convivial family outings. Iron ore mining and petrochemicals have left scars on the landscape near Cartagena, while overfishing and toxic waste endanger marine life. Expanding hotel complexes and new roads required to meet the demands of international tourism are damaging fauna and flora along the coast, and huge satellite towns for tourists *(urbanizaciones)* are guzzling precious fresh water. However, some areas have been designated *parques naturales* and so enjoy special status.

FIRE AND WATER

Every year it's the same. During the summer, along the whole of the Spanish coast, people pray for rain and curse the catastrophic fires, which regularly lay waste huge areas of land. In 1994, in the province of València alone, 160,000 hectares (about 400,000 acres) of pine forest were destroyed. In 2000 much of the Parque Natural del Montgó was burnt in a fire that raged for a week. The severe water shortages, which have existed for years now, are changing the face of the landscape. During the summer of 2001, drinking water had to be rationed in the popular tourist resort of the Xàbia.

Many people are now linking the *sequía*, the great drought, to changes in the world climate, but environmentalists also point to other contributory factors. The southern Spanish golf courses, for example, soak up as much water as the Spanish capital, a city of 5 million people.

Below: thirsty golf course
Bottom: family fun in València

The pine forests, planted in grand style in the 1950s, are also causing problems. These cheap conifers grow rapidly and bring easy profits to the forestry companies, but monocultures such as this make the soil more susceptible to erosion and landslides. In addition, the resin in the pine trees burns like tinder, and unlike the native deciduous trees, conifers do not regrow after a fire.

POPULATION

Of the 40 million or so Spaniards, some 5 million live in the autonomous regions of València and Murcia. Comunitat Valenciana boasts a population of just over 4 million inhabitants, Comunidad Murcia 1.1 million. València is Spain's third largest city and the most densely populated area

(2,050 people per sq km/5,309 per sq mile), while in the Maestrazgo region there are only 14 people per sq km (36 per sq mile).

The urban centres have long drawn in country dwellers, and 78 percent of the population now live in the coastal conurbations. Rural depopulation has a long tradition in these parts. In the early 20th century, farmers left their villages in droves and headed for the coast, where industry and tourism offered some future prospects.

Below: young woman in Murcia
Bottom: veterans in Cartagena

But not all the new arrivals were able to make a living there either, and in the 1950s and 1960s many left for Catalonia, France or Germany. At the same time, jobseekers from Andalusia settled in València or Murcia; many found work in the iron ore mines near Cartagena.

The coastal zone is currently experiencing further growth from Moroccan guest workers, retired people and other 'part-time Spaniards' seeking refuge from chilly northern European winters.

In line with the trend throughout Spain, and contrary to the commonly-held view that southern Europeans have large families, the birth rate is falling and stands at just 1.18 children per mother here which parallels the national average. By the coast, 20 percent of the population is below the age of 16, while many of the inland villages are populated almost entirely by the over-sixties. Thanks to *Turismo de Interior*, which promotes

tourism away from the beaches, the regional governments can now promise better prospects for the younger generation.

IDENTITY

The Spanish have a strong sense of regional loyalty, and this is often heard in their fondness for puns and in light-hearted mockery of fellow countrymen from other regions or cities. *Antes marrano que murciano* (better a pig than a Murcian) and *Toledano, tonto y vano* (Toledans, stupid and vain) are good examples of this sort of talk; they live on more because of the rhyme and the sound, than out of any genuine belief in their content.

The typical qualities ascribed to the *Valenciano* are worldliness and a zest for life, but also self-righteousness and small-mindedness; both these strands probably have more to do with the long-standing trading traditions of the coastal inhabitants. Rural, provincial qualities such as hard work, toughness and a realistic approach to life are usually attributed to the *Murciano* – but very few people take these clichés too seriously.

THE LANGUAGE

After such international events as the 1992 Olympics and the 2002 Year of Gaudí (both in Barcelona), the world suddenly became aware that Castilian Spanish or *castellano* is not the only language spoken in Spain. The Catalans used such occasions to promote their regional identity. What was not always made clear, however, is that the Catalan language is also spoken in the province of València. In fact, Catalan is an official language here, although the dialect spoken in València is known as Valenciano *(Valencià)*.

Spanish traffic signs are frequently daubed with independence slogans and most museums stick to the Catalan language to describe their exhibits, but on a day-to-day level, people's choice of language is not an article of faith. Unlike many Catalans, when Valencians talk to visitors, they can quickly change between Castilian Spanish and Valenciano.

Role of religion
While it is true that Spain is a Catholic country, the official religion is losing influence in everyday life. Only 30 percent of all Spaniards describe themselves as practising Catholics. But everyone seems to get involved with the lively, church-initiated celebrations – and there is certainly no shortage of these in València and Murcia.

Sign in Alicante

Sign language

Because of the unusual language situation in València, you might see *playa* (Spanish for beach) in one place, and somewhere else you will see *platja* (Catalan); *rio* (Spanish for river) is often – but not always – spelled *riu* (Catalan), and so on. But don't let this worry you. Whether you read ¡Bienvenido en Alicante! or ¡Benvingut en Alacant!, it means the same thing: visitors are very welcome.

Financial powerhouse in València

Both spellings for many streets and squares are perfectly acceptable. Valenciano is most widely used in the rural areas along the coast between Vinaròs in the north and Torrevieja in the south. It is actually now rare to hear Valenciano being spoken in the towns, and even in the mountain regions Castilian is the language of everyday use.

THE ECONOMY

Agriculture equals 17 percent of exports from the Comunidad and València and Murcia are the most productive market gardens in the whole of Europe. One in 10 jobs depend on agricultural exports. Irrigation techniques introduced by the Arabs are used to collect every drop of water in this fertile alluvial land *(see page 19)*. The Spanish Levant is responsible for 80 percent of Spain's citrus fruit crops. Thanks to the irrigation channels and the climate, crops of tomatoes, peppers, artichokes, aubergines, pomegranates, melons, rice, wheat and other agricultural produce are harvested three times, sometimes more, per year.

Since Spain joined the European Union, the industrialisation of agriculture has continued apace. Most farmland in the Levant was traditionally geared towards self-sufficiency, and in most cases the estates are too small for efficient production. So the old farmhouses *(barracas)* are giving way to modern, purpose-built units and greenhouses, where the profitable early crops are grown for export. The continuing drought and rising demand for water from the main plantations, in Murcia in particular, has prompted a change to the cultivation of olives, almonds and grapes.

Industry also plays an important role in the Levant these days. After Barcelona, València is the largest centre for automobile construction and heavy engineering by the Mediterranean. Textile factories are found in Alcoi, shoes and leather goods are manufactured in Elx and elsewhere. Fishing and fish processing, on the other hand, are now not so important. Artisans continue the Moorish tradition of pottery making, enamelling and glass making. Clay tiles painted with colourful designs (*azulejos* from the Arabic *az-zulaych*) and pots are popular souvenirs from València.

The Sierra de Cartagena is well endowed with minerals (copper, tin, lead, silver), but the last mines near La Unión were closed in 1991, when they ceased to be profitable.

The unemployment rate in Murcia and València is about 11 percent. This is well below the Spanish average, with mainly young people among those unable to find work.

TOURISM

The dominant economic stimulus in Murcia and València is undoubtedly tourism – including residential. In 2002 foreigners invested some 560 million euros in the purchase of second homes in Spain, especially on the 'Costas'. In 2002 also some 8 million tourists visited the Levant coast plus many Spanish holiday makers annually spend the hot summer months in their holiday apartments by the sea.

About 45 percent of those in work are in the service and tourist trades. The negative consequences of the construction boom can still be seen in some places. Hotel overcapacity in the 1980s led to bankruptcies, so entrepreneurs in the tourist sector are cautiously diversifying. Now it is not just the beach resorts, so popular during the summer,

Below: wares for sale, València central market
Bottom: tourists in Peníscola

but also towns in the interior, which are profiting from the rising number of visitors – and, whenever possible, on a year-round basis.

POLITICS AND ADMINISTRATION

When the Franco era ended with the death of the dictator in 1975, the reactionary, centralised state was transformed into a pluralist federation of historically mature regions. València and Murcia are just two of a total of 17 autonomous regions. Independent of Madrid, their parliaments make decisions about culture, education and tourism.

Below: València's Palau de la Generalitat
Bottom: València town hall

For administrative purposes, Spain is divided into 50 provinces. In the case of Murcia, the autonomous region and the province are identical, whereas the Comunitat Valenciana is divided into three *provincias*: Castelló, València and Alacant. The provincial councillors are elected from the municipalities *(municipios)*, who, together with the regional parliament, despatch representatives to the Senate (Upper House) in the bicameral National Assembly *(Cortes Generales)* in Madrid. The Lower House in the *Cortes* is made up of deputies directly elected by the people.

The dominant political force in Spain from 1982 to 1996 was the PSOE *(Partido Socialista Obrero Español)* under Prime Minister Felipe González. The Socialists introduced a social

welfare system with unemployment pay, pensions and sickness benefits. They built motorways, promoted women's rights and removed from the constitution backward-looking moral codes.

Since 1996, the national government has been led with a small majority by the PP *(Partido Popular)* under Prime Minister José María Aznar, who domestically espouses liberalisation and privatisation policies. In regional elections in València and Murcia, the Conservatives usually lead the field. For example, in the most recent regional elections held in May 2003, the PP won 48 seats (53.9 percent) and the PSOE won 36 seats (40.4 percent). The third force in Spanish politics is the *Izquierda Unida* (IU), a left-wing alliance that poses little competition.

THE MOORISH LEGACY

València and Murcia's wealth from farming is due mainly to the invading Moors, who between the 8th and 11th centuries introduced many new plants to the Iberian peninsula. Their names reveal their Arab origins, e.g. the Spanish for rice is *arroz* from the Arabic *arruzz*, an orange is *naranja* from *narandj*, and an apricot *albaricoque* from *al-barqûq*. The Arabs also provided the rootstock for the huge plantations of date palms in Elx and Orihuela. Even the olive, a common sight round the Mediterranean, is an import from the Middle East.

Their greatest contribution was in irrigation. The Islamic engineers perfected the techniques devised earlier by the Romans. Using a system of locks and artificial canals *(vegas)*, Moorish farmers flooded the fields with precisely measured quantities of river or spring water. Where the natural land contours were insufficient to distribute the water, beasts of burden lifted the liquid to the required level using waterwheels *(norias)*.

The Museo de la Huerta in Alcantarilla *(see page 88)* illustrates the traditional farming methods. Motorised pumps now do the work formerly done by mules, and the old *vegas* have been concreted over – but, basically, little has been done to improve on the Moorish principles.

El Cid (1043–99)

No historical figure better encapsulates the changing and confusing history of the Christian *reconquista* than Rodrigo Díaz de Vivar, popularly known as El Cid (from the Arabic *sejjid* meaning lord).

Born in 1043 in the town of Vivar near Burgos, in his early years as a knight he won the title of *campeador* (fighter). He married the niece of the Christian King Alfonso VI, but was banished from Castile because of his involvement in courtly intrigues.

The outcast switched allegiances to fight for the Moors. But in 1087, when Alfonso called on him for help, he rejoined the Christian cause. He then went on to liberate eastern Spain from Moorish danger.

In Maestrazgo, one or two place names still evoke the popular war hero. In 1094, El Cid captured València for the Christians, ruling it until his death in 1099. He and his wife are buried in Burgos cathedral.

Every schoolchild knows the story of El Cid. The anonymous epic *El Cantar de mío Cid* (1140) immortalises him as a hero of the *reconquista*.

El Cid, the Moor slayer

HISTORICAL HIGHLIGHTS

Early times Evidence of human settlement dating back to 20,000BC has been discovered on the Spanish Mediterranean coast. Countless cave paintings from this era have survived, notably in Maestrazgo.

About 4000BC The Iberians, a tribe related to the North African Berbers, settled here.

About 2000BC In the quest for metal deposits, Phoenicians established settlements near Orihuela.

7th centuryBC Greek traders set up bases around the modern towns of Sagunt, Benidorm and Alicante.

From 250BC Carthaginian armies under Hasdrubal conquer large parts of Spain.

219BC Hannibal conquers Saguntum (modern Sagunt), a town allied with Rome, triggering the Second Punic War between Carthage and Rome.

200BC–AD14 The Romans defeat the Carthaginians, colonise Spain and impose their culture on the land. Valentia Edetanorum (València) is one of the Roman settlements.

From 711 Roman Hispania, previously overrun by the Visigoths, is now almost completely occupied by Moorish armies from North Africa.

8th–11th century The religiously tolerant Moors make a huge contribution to the peninsula's culture. During the 11th century, the Christian kingdoms in the north gradually advance south, fighting to regain land from the Moors. The Christian Reconquest (*reconquista*) fragments the Caliphate into isolated principalities. After the fall of Toledo in 1085, the struggle became increasingly a holy war between Christians and Muslims.

1094 El Cid conquers València.

1238 Jaume I of Aragón takes València and Murcia, but València is granted autonomy as an independent kingdom.

1266 Murcia falls to Castile under the rule of Alfonso X.

1469 The marriage between Fernando II, crown prince of Aragón, and Isabel I of Castile ('the Catholic monarchs'), unites the two kingdoms.

1480 Authorised by a papal bull, the Spanish Inquisition is set up by Fernando and Isabel under the Inquisitor General Tomás de Torquemada. Those suspected of heresy were persecuted to ensure the religious unity of the country.

1492 The Christian *reconquista* ends with the conquest of Granada, the Moors' last bastion in Spain. Jews and converted Moors *(moriscos)* are banished or persecuted with renewed vigour. Isabel gives her support to Christopher Columbus, whose voyage of discovery prepares the way for the establishment of the Spanish colonial empire in Central and South America.

15th century Commercial prosperity throughout the kingdom of València based on manufacturing, the silk trade and banking.

1519–23 The uprising of Valencian guilds against the Inquisition and the nobility is violently suppressed.

1588 Defeat of the Spanish Armada: its 133-ship fleet is destroyed in an attempt to invade Protestant England.

1609 Felipe III orders the expulsion of the last Moors (about 500,000) still living in southern Spain and València.

1701–13 In the War of the Spanish Succession, the Bourbon Philip of Anjou, grandson of the French king Louis XIV, defeats the Austrians under Charles, Duke of Habsburg. The kingdom of València is annexed by the Castilians.

1812 The first Spanish constitution is adopted.

1833–9 The first of three Carlist Wars: in the power struggle for succession to Fernando VII, València sides with his brother, Don Carlos.

1851 Concordat with the Pope confirms the exclusive status of the Roman Catholic religion in Spain.

1873 Proclamation of the First Republic by dictator Emilio Castelar; bloody revolts in Cartagena.

1890 Universal suffrage is introduced.

1923 Military dictatorship by General Primero de Rivera following a putsch.

1936–9 The Spanish Civil War devastates the country, claiming 1.2 million lives. València is the seat of the Republican Popular Front government. Alicante and Murcia remain Republican. The Civil War ends with the fall of Madrid and surrender to the Nationalists.

1939–45 During World War II Spain remains neutral.

1939–75 Spain is run by 'El Caudillo', the dictator General Francisco Franco.

1945 By the end of World War II, Spain finds itself diplomatically and politically isolated.

1953 A deal with the US permits American bases on Spanish soil in return for economic and military aid worth a billion dollars.

1955 Spain joins the United Nations.

1959 Founding of the Basque separatist group ETA.

1975 Franco dies and Spain becomes a parliamentary monarchy under King Juan Carlos I. Catalan, Basque and Galician are recognised as official languages.

1977 First free elections return centrist government under Adolfo Suarez. The Communist Party (PCE) is legalised.

1982 A landslide electoral victory brings the Socialist Workers Party (PSOE) under Felipe González to power. The regions of València and Murcia gain autonomous status (Alicante becomes València's southern province). Spain joins NATO.

1986 Spain joins the European Community (later the European Union), a process completed in 1992.

1992 500th anniversary of Christopher Columbus's voyage of discovery. The Barcelona Olympics and Seville Expo '92 place Spain firmly within the community of modern nations. The country's first high-speed train link opens between Seville and Madrid.

1996 José María Aznar (PP) replaces Felipe González as President.

2000 José María Aznar (PP) is re-elected President.

2002 On 1 January the euro replaced the Spanish peseta as the sole currency.

2003 Against popular opinion, Aznar supports the US war in Iraq.

Map on page 26

Previous page: La Vila Joiosa
Below: València street tile
Bottom: the town hall

1: València

The name *La Clara* or 'the whiteness', as the Levant's capital city is sometimes known, derives from the soft Mediterranean sunlight, which bathes the city. But do not be fooled into thinking that València is all about radiance and fun. The city has grown to its present size because of the down-to-earth nature of its inhabitants, through trade and industry. The Gothic splendour of the old town, with its symbol – the bell tower El Micalet – testifies to the self-confidence of the early Valencian merchants. Tourist highlights such as La Llotja, the old silk market, and the bustling produce market are other examples of València's commercial vitality.

Culturally, València has plenty to offer, including the stunning City of Arts and Sciences, the IVAM art gallery and the ultra-modern Palau de la Música concert-hall. The city is also renowned for its long nights – visitors arriving here for the famous *Las Fallas* fiesta should be ready for an endurance test.

HISTORY

Founded in 138BC under the Roman name of Valentia Edetanorum and governed from 714 by Arabs, València became an important *taifa* or independent kingdom, whose wealth derived from farming and trade. In 1094, El Cid *(see page 19)* elevated the town to capital of a Christian principality, but in 1102 València was reoccupied by Islamic troops. As was the case elsewhere in Spain, Arab dominance meant religious tolerance, and Christians, Jews and Muslims co-existed in peace. This did not change when Jaume I ('the Conqueror') brought the Arab era to an end in 1238. He tied València to the union of Aragon and Catalonia, thus guaranteeing the kingdom a degree of autonomy.

During the 15th century, under the influence of the business-oriented Catalans, València developed into an important trading centre. Starting out in 1407 as a trading exchange, La Llotja bourse went on to become an international meeting place for silk, textile and ceramics traders. But with the discovery of the New World, the towns and cities on the Atlantic coast gained in importance at the expense of the Mediterranean ports, and then the centralised powers in Madrid abolished the city's special privileges, despite some determined resistance by the Valencian moneyed classes. The expulsion of the converted Moors (*moriscos*), whose talents played a major part in creating the city's prosperity, marked the end of València's 'Golden Age'.

Over the next 500 years, the Valencians rebelled repeatedly and in vain against Castilian and French oppressors; in fact, during the Spanish Civil War (1936–39), it was the seat of the Republican government. Now València is Spain's third largest city and home to around 800,000 people. Its commercial importance as the third force, after Madrid and Barcelona, continues to increase.

AROUND EL MICALET

The ★★ **Catedral de Santa Maria ❶** exhibits a variety of styles. It was started in 1262 in Gothic form on the foundations of an Arab mosque. The extravagantly arching main portal, the **Puerta de los Hierros**, designed in the early 18th century by the German pupil of Bernini, Konrad Rudolf,

Star Attraction
● Catedral de Santa Maria

Parking
València is not by the sea. The harbour (El Grao) and the local beach (La Malvarrosa) are situated some 6km (4 miles) from the old town, the Ciutat Vella. It is impossible to park in the old quarter, so leave your car in one of the many carparks, or by the ring road beside the dried-up Riu Túria. The city centre is only a few minutes' walk away from the main station (Estació del Nord).

València's cathedral

Map below

is pure Baroque. In contrast, late 18th-century classical elements dominate in the side chapels.

The octagonal **Miguelete** bell tower (open Tues–Sun 10am–12.30pm, 4.30–6.30pm), offers a magnificent panoramic view over València. The viewing terrace at a height of 51m (167ft) is at the top of the narrow spiral staircase with 207 steps.

The illustrated panels by the high altar inside the church are of special interest. Two pupils of Leonardo da Vinci, Fernando Yáñez and Fernando de Llanos, painted these scenes from the life of the Virgin Mary between 1507 and 1509. An agate cup, said to be the Holy Grail (*Santo Cáliz*), the mysterious object sought by King

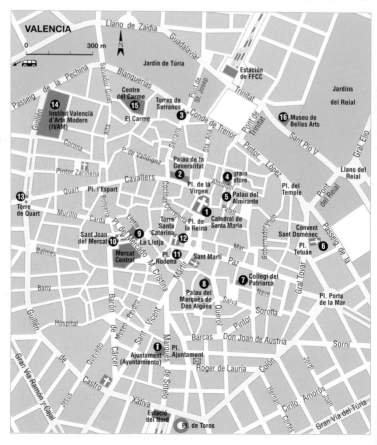

Arthur and his knights, is kept in the Gothic **Capilla de Santo Cáliz**. As well as two paintings by Goya (1799), the **Museu de la Catedral** (open Mon–Sat 10am–1pm, 4.30–7pm), which adjoins the chapel, displays a magnificently ornate 4-m (13-ft) high monstrance (20th century).

PUERTA DE LOS APOSTOLES

The narrow Calle Miguelete passage to the left of the cathedral leads to the ★ **Puerta de los Apóstoles**. Here, every Thursday at midday, a unique court, the **Water Tribunal,** meets beneath the Gothic rose window on the west portal.

Eight men dressed in black, plus an usher (*alguacil*), assemble in front of the Puerta de los Apóstoles to impose the law. Judgements are delivered orally, there is no appeal and they apply immediately. However, no one need fear lynch justice, because there are no capital crimes at stake here. The *Tribunal de las Aguas* is the only one of its kind in the world. Its job, which it has been performing for 1,000 years, is to settle disputes between the farmers who draw water from València's eight irrigation canals (*acequías*). Offenders are punished with fines or temporary loss of water. The spectacle is witnessed by many onlookers who are amazed at the short time the session lasts. The *alguacil* simply calls out the names of the eight irrigation zones and, because there are usually no complaints, the court ends – until next Thursday at noon.

PLAZA DE LA VIRGEN

The ★★ **Plaza de la Virgen** square is the traditional meeting place for Valencians. On a hot day it is hard to resist the temptation of a refreshing drink at one of the square's outdoor cafés. Countless white doves swoop and flutter beside the Riu Túria fountain in the middle of the square.

A small chamber behind the altar in the domed **Basílica de la Mare de Deú dels Desemparats** (1667), linked to the cathedral with an arch, is the home of a small statue of the Madonna (14th

Star Attraction
● Plaza de la Virgen

Artist's inspiration
The Valencian Impressionist painter Joaquín Soller, who is best known for his brilliantly lit Mediterranean beaches, was inspired by the light of La Malvarossa beach, east of the city.

Below: cathedral interior
Bottom: Plaza de la Virgen

Map on page 26

👁 **Ones that get away…** Hundreds of artists and craftsmen labour all year round to build the elaborate *ninots*, papier-mâché figures that are set alight during Valencia's festival of *Las Fallas (see page 104)*. Some figures are voted too good for burning, and are saved to be displayed in the Museu Fallero on Plaza Monteolivete.

century). During the *Las Fallas* festivities, the city's poor come here to pay homage to València's patron, known as the Virgin of the Helpless.

Opposite stands the ★ **Palau de la Generalitat ❷**, a Gothic palace dating from the 15th century. This seat of the València regional government is a powerful symbol of the region's autonomy. Unfortunately, it is not open to the public.

NORTH AND EAST OF THE PLAZA

To the north of Plaza de la Virgen, the impressive twin towers known as ★ **Torres de Serranos ❸**, part of an earlier city gate (1398), mark the boundary of medieval València. To the east of the Desamparados church, the Arabic **grain store ❹** *(Almudí, Valencian also Almoina)*, dating from the 14th century, testifies to València's importance as a trading city.

Follow the narrow alleyways past the grand **Palau del Almirante ❺** (note the patio with an attractive staircase) to the Gothic **San Juan del Hospital** church and the former **Convent Sant Domènec ❻**, now part of an army barracks. To view the church and the magnificent ★ **Capella dels Reis**, make an appointment with the guards.

Palau del Marquès de Dos Aigües

COLLEGI DEL PATRIARCA

The ★ **Collegi del Patriarca ❼**, formerly a seminary built in the severe Renaissance style of the mid-16th century, has a perfect courtyard with 56 Carrara marble columns. The ★★ **gallery** has a collection of mainly Spanish religious paintings from the 15th to the 17th centuries, including works by El Greco and Ribalta (open daily 11am–1.30pm). On the opposite side of the road stands the university's original building (19th century).

PALAU DOS AIGÜES

The vast, ornate, playful facade for the ★★ **Palau del Marquès de Dos Aigües ❽**, a late-Baroque palace (1740), is initially reminiscent of art nouveau style. The alabaster portal crowned by a mother of God is flanked by two muscular figures on overturned water jugs, Riu Túria and Riu Júcar, who symbolise the marquis's title (Catalan *dos aigües:* two waters). The theme of running water is continued with creepers, garlands and palm trees, which flow over the windows and cornices. The painter and sculptor, Hipólito Rovira Brocandel, who designed the palace facade, died a tormented soul in 1765.

The ★★ **Museu Nacional de Cerámica** ceramics museum (open Tues–Sat 10am–2pm, 4–8pm, Sun/public holidays 10am–2pm) includes outstanding works by Manises, Paterna and Alcora.

MERCANTILE VALENCIA

The central square in the southern part of the old town is the wedge-shaped **Plaça de l'Ajuntament**. Surrounding it are impressive business premises, colourful flower stands and the classical-style **town hall** (1921). On the ground floor, the **Museu Històric Municipal** (open Mon–Fri 9am–2pm) has various national symbols such as the *senyera*, València's first flag, and the decree of autonomous rights granted by Jaume I.

To the south of Plaça de l'Ajuntament, the busy Avenida Marqués de Sotelo leads to the colossal **bullfighting arena** (1860), with the Museu

Star Attractions
● Collegi del Patriarca gallery
● Palau del Marquès
de Dos Aigües
● Museu González Martí

Below: Plaça Colegio del Patriarca
Bottom: Plaça de l'Ajuntament

Map
on page
26

Taurino and also the **main station** *(Estació del Nord)* in an interesting art deco style.

MARKETS

Take the **Avenida María Cristina**, to the north of Plaça de l'Ajuntament, as far as **Plaça del Mercat**, the heart of the city's business quarter. Outside the entrance to the market are several popular street cafés, which serve market-fresh canapés.

València's main market, ★★**El Mercat Central**, is a remarkable feast for the senses. Beneath two airy iron and glass domes, made in 1928 under the banner of *modernisme*, everything that the sea, the mountains and, of course, the *huerta* yields up, is traded here. Myriad aromas, cheerful banter and throngs of people fill the halls, with the glass roofs dispersing the sunlight like a church window. The only difference is that this cathedral is closed on Sunday.

★★**La Llotja ❾**, a splendid Gothic building, testifies to the townsfolk's entrepreneurial spirit and their second religion, which is the worship of money (open Tues–Sat 9.15am–2pm, 4.30–8pm, Sun 9.15am–2pm). With its magnificent rose windows, La Llotja (also known as *Lonja de la Seda* or the Silk Exchange) radiates with an almost sacred dignity, but as a commodities exchange it was only ever used for secular purposes. Silk

Time for a drink…
The best *horchata de chufa* (tiger nut milk) has been prepared at the Horchatería El Siglo on Plaça Santa Caterina since 1836. Another pleasant place to linger is at the rear of the exchange by the Plaça de Doctor Collado, where the long-established El Kiosco bar serves hearty tapas. In the Barri Cabañal, Bodega Montaña (Calle José Benlliure 69, tel: 963 67 23 14; $) is full of happily swigging locals and has great tapas.

La Llotja

used to be exchanged in the main chamber *(Sala de la Contratación)*, where bankers, ship owners and businessmen would gather. Some 20 slender columns, supporting the 36-m (118-ft) long ceiling, converge to form a vault-like structure resembling elegant date palms. The room is now used as an exhibition and event centre. The **Consolat de Mar**, added on to the Llotja in 1548, was the seat of the Maritime Court and the first chamber of commerce.

Directly opposite the commodities exchange is the Gothic **Sant Joan del Mercat** ❿ (1368), which was badly damaged during the Spanish Civil War. In the middle of the maze of alleyways to the east of the Llotja is the circular ★ **Plaça Rodona** ⓫, a bazaar, where under a sunroof shops sell embroidery, fabrics, souvenirs and bric-à-brac. On Sunday morning, it is the setting for a small flea market. Behind it, almost on Plaça de la Reina, rises the Baroque ★ **Torre Santa Caterina** ⓬ (1688). This church's bell tower is one of the finest in the Levant.

EL CARME

Calle Bolsería leads into the old town district of ★ **El Carme**. It is worth taking a stroll through this former red-light district to savour the atmosphere of the lively street cafés and bars, such as those by Plaça de l'Espart. It is not just dusty junk shops and tiny workshops that characterise this district; it is decaying houses, crumbling plaster and debris along the narrow alleyways. The city authorities are planning a major facelift for El Carme.

Calle de Quart on the left ends at the second, surviving city gate, where threatening fortress towers, the ★ **Torres de Quart** ⓭ (15th century), resemble outsize chess pieces. Calle Caballeros leads back to Plaza de la Virgen *(see page 27).*

ART AND CULTURE BY THE RIU TURIA

After the catastrophic floods of 1957, the river course to the south of the town was covered over and the bed of the tamed Túria incorporated into

Star Attractions
● El Mercat Central
● La Llotja

Below: El Mercat Central
Bottom: Torres de Quart

Map on page 26

Museu de Belles Arts

Spectacular symbol

To mark the beginning of a new millennium, València acquired a new symbol: the ★ **Ciutat de les Arts i de les Ciènces** or the 'City of Arts and Sciences', designed by Santiago Calatrava.

The **Hemisfèric**, a planetarium and an IMAX cinema in the form of a giant eye made from reinforced concrete, was actually opened in 1998. After that came a high-tech and art museum as well as an oceanography park (20 minutes by car on the *autovía* to El Saler southeast of València). Take a virtual tour at www.cac.es

the modern city as a park. Ricard Bofill, the architect responsible for some of Barcelona's Olympic sites, created the new layout.

The ultra-modern ★ **Institut Valencià d'Arte Modern (IVAM) ⑭**, opened in 1989, houses works by Juli Gonzàlez, Ignacio Pinazo and Antoni Tàpies, among others (open Tues–Sun 10am–8pm). Temporary exhibitions are held in the neighbouring **Centre del Carme ⑮**, a Carmelite convent with a fine cloister.

On the other bank, across the Pont de la Trinitat (1402), the ★★ **Museu de Belles Arts ⑯** has a collection of works by Velázquez, Goya, El Greco and Hieronymus Bosch, as well as Valencian masters such as Ribalta and Ribera (open Tues–Sun 10am–2pm, Tues–Sat 4–6pm). Adjoining the museum is the **Jardins del Reial** (also known as Vivers), a park with an avenue of palm trees and an ornamental pond.

Two other crossings, built in the late 16th century, Pont del Reial and Pont de la Mar, connect the old and new town. The asymmetric silhouette of Santiago Calatrava's modern arch bridge forms a delightful contrast. Equally futuristic is the ★ **Palau de la Música** (1989), which is noted for its classical concerts. For information about events, call 963 37 50 20.

CONGRESS HALL

The post-modern **Palacio de Congresos**, designed by the top British architect Norman Foster (on Gran Vía de les Corts Valencianes), is one of the most successful congress halls in Spain. Take bus number 10 or 11 from the town hall *(Ajuntament)*. For trade fair information, contact València Convention Bureau, Carmelitas 1, tel: 963 60 63 53, fax: 963 60 64 30, www.turisvalencia.es

EXCURSIONS

València's beaches do not always look that inviting, so at weekends it is better to make for **La Malvarrosa** (1km/½ mile to the north of El Grao harbour) or **El Saler** (5km/3 miles to the south)

and observe scenes from everyday Spanish life: rampaging children, harassed parents, grandmothers in black, blaring radios… Several buses and a local train run to La Malvarrosa; El Saler can be reached by bus (from Estació del Nord).

Beach restaurants (known in Spanish as *chiringuitos*), such as **Las Arenas** and **La Pepica** in La Malvarrosa, keep day-trippers well supplied with paella and seafood at reasonable prices, while at night **La Champañería** nightclub offers sparkling wine and dancing (summer only).

Better-quality fish restaurants are to be found on the north side of the harbour – for example, **L'Estimat** on Avenida Neptuno *(see page 111)*.

BIRD SANCTUARY

Beyond El Saler 15km (9 miles) to the south of València lies ★ **L'Albufera** bird sanctuary, a habitat for little egret, ducks and herons. Despite a conservation order issued in 1986, the area still faces a threat from sewage, fertilisers and natural silting. The ★ **Racó de l'Olla** visitor centre (with viewing tower, close-circuit TV cameras and nature trail) illustrates how the area of the lake, which during the 19th century covered 15,000 hectares (37,000 acres), had by 1995 shrunk to 2,500 hectares (6,200 acres), and allows you to view the wildlife without disturbing them.

Star Attraction
● Museu de Belles Arts

Below: Convent del Carme
Bottom: Jardins del Reial

Below: Peníscola view
Bottom: Cantavieja in the Maestrazgo

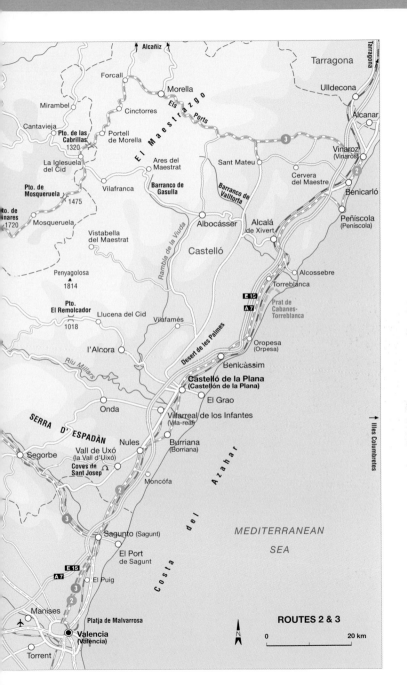

ROUTES 2 & 3

0   20 km

Map
on pages
34-5

2: Costa del Azahar

València – Sagunt – Castelló – Orpesa del Mar – Peníscola – Vinaròs (160km/100 miles)

Cynics deride the resorts along the 'Orange Blossom Coast' as nothing but concessions to mass tourism, but away from the apartment and hotel complexes, snack bars and advertising hoardings, there is still room for some Mediterranean charm. The historic 'old-town' centres, in many of the settlements between the Ebro delta and València, provide visitors with a fascinating contrast to the beach. And if you're travelling in the spring and you keep the windows open, then the exquisite scent from the roadside plantations will accompany your travels. Allow two days to complete this route along the Costa del Azahar.

Below: Sagunt ceramic shop
Bottom: Castillo

EL PUIG

Leave València in a northerly direction on the N-340 (extension of the Avenida de la Constitución) or on the A-7 toll motorway (via Gran Vía de Marqués de Túria). After 18km (11 miles) you will reach **El Puig** ('the hill'), where a ruined castle dating from the *reconquista* towers above the small *huerta* settlement.

To commemorate his victories, Jaume I founded the **Santa María del Puig** monastery in 1237,

dedicating it to the patron saint of the kingdom of València. Since then, it has been occupied by monks from the Mercedarian order, who traditionally attend the Spanish royal family when they stay in València.

Housed in one wing of the fortress-like building is an interesting printing and graphics museum (**Museo de Imprenta y Obra Gráfica**).

At the weekends, the beaches at **Puebla de Farnals** (14km/9 miles from València) attract many day-trippers from the nearby towns.

SAGUNT

Seen from the main road, the town of ★ **Sagunt** (pop. 57,000) by the Río Palancia looks distinctly unattractive. Faceless apartment blocks predominate alongside industrial sites and abandoned steelworks. The noisy through traffic on the main highway adds to the grim picture. Yet it is worth taking time to explore the ★ **Ciutat Vella**, which has a history extending back 3,000 years.

TEATRO ROMANO AND CASTILLO

First park your car on Plaza Cronista Chabret (also known as La Glorieta) and then take a stroll past the town hall *(Casa Consistorial)*, across Plaza Mayor with its medieval colonnades (market on Wednesday), to the castle hill.

Until they were driven out by the Inquisition, Sephardic Jews inhabited the maze of alleyways in the **Barrio de la Judería** on the right-hand side. Calle Castillo ascends steeply to the ★ **Teatro Romano** *(for opening times see Castillo, below)*. The Roman amphitheatre (2nd century) has seating for some 4,000 spectators, and now, after a full-scale facelift including new lighting, it is again being used for summer concerts and plays.

The ★ **Castillo** (also known as Acrópolis), built on a ridge of the Sierra Calderona, consists of seven divisions or plazas, which offer magnificent views of the town and surrounding countryside (open Tues–Sat 10am–dusk, Sun 10am–2pm). Iberians, Carthaginians, Romans, Arabs, Valencian

Ancient Saguntum
In 219BC, in spite of eight months of fierce resistance by its inhabitants, the 28-year-old Carthaginian general Hannibal finally conquered ancient Saguntum. As they preferred death by fire to imprisonment, the townsfolk torched all the houses. This horrifying event served as a trigger for the Second Punic War, during which Sagunt was recaptured by the Romans and rebuilt.

Sagunt old town

Map
on pages
34–5

Republicans, whoever was in charge in Sagunt, left their own characteristic mark on the 1-km (½-mile) long castle complex perched above the town. There is a small archaeological museum within the complex.

Walk back down to the town centre along the cypress-lined Way of the Cross, ★ **El Calvario** (19th century), the route taken by Sagunt's Good Friday procession.

South of Plaza Mayor in the town itself, the remains of the **Templo de Diana** (5th century BC), spared by Hannibal when he conquered Saguntum, and the early Gothic church of **San Salvador** (13th century) close to the railway station, are worth closer inspection.

Below: El Calvario
Bottom: Coves de Sant Josep

Most of the Sagunt municipality lies about 3km (2 miles) away by the sea. **El Port de Sagunt's** 15km (9 miles) of sandy beach, plus restaurants, cafés and discotheques, make for a lively scene during the summer months.

COVES DE SANT JOSEP

Near Nules, the C-225 turns off into the interior. Just beyond Vall d'Uixó, signposts point to ★ **Coves de Sant Josep**. A tributary of the Riu Belcaide runs underground for some 2,384m (7,820ft), and in the process it has formed a complex of caves that was explored for the first

time only in the 1920s. Almost a kilometre (½ mile) of the illuminated, underground water-course can be explored on a 40-minute boat ride (in summer months, daily 11am–1.30pm and 3.30–6.30pm, otherwise at irregular times; tel: 964 69 05 76; www.riosubterraneo.com).

VILA-REAL

The town of **Vila-real** (pop. 38,000) lies amid the fields of oranges cultivated on the fertile *huerta* of the Plana Baixa district. It is worth making a detour to view the huge 17th-century **Sant Jaume** church, whose octagonal Baroque tower dominates the town centre. Vila-real, like the neighbouring towns of Onda, Ribesalbes and Alcora (12km/7 miles to the west), is noted for its traditional pottery.

> **Oranges, the only fruit**
> A short distance from Vila-real, at **Burriana,** south of the Riu Millars, the **Museu de la Taronja** (Orange Museum; Calle Major 10) provides an illuminating insight into the cultivation, processing and marketing of the Valencian national fruit (open Tues–Sat 10am–1pm, Sun 10am–2pm).

Castelló cathedral

CASTELLO

Compared to either Alicante or València, **Castelló** (pop. 142,000), the capital of the eponymous province, still looks rather like an overgrown village, despite the sizeable modern quarter. The last part of its official name, Castelló de la Plana (in the plain), refers to the flat *huerta* that surrounds the town. In 1938, during the Spanish Civil War, Franco's army bombed its way through to the Mediterranean, and this town, which was founded in the 13th century by Jaume I, suffered terrible damage. Now Castelló is a trading centre for vegetables from the *huerta* and citrus fruits, and the port is used for the export of ceramic and porcelain products.

PLAZA MAYOR

At the heart of the old town lies Plaza Mayor, around which the main sights are clustered. Only the portals of the 16th-century **Catedral de Santa María** survived the ravages of the civil war; the rest of the building was faithfully rebuilt in the original Gothic style. The 58-m (190-ft) free-standing bell tower, known as ★ **El Fadrí** (The

Map on pages 34–5

Nature park
Illes Columbretes, an archipelago of uninhabited volcanic islands about 60km (37 miles) off Castelló, was designated as a nature park in 1988. Some local companies organise boat trips to the main island of **Columbrete Grande**. Rare birds nest amid the sparse vegetation of this 68-m (223-ft) high horseshoe-shaped rock, and in the clear water it is usually possible to pick out crayfish, corals and moray eels.

Below and bottom:
Museu de Belles Arts, Castello

Apprentice), has become a symbol for the town. The highly ornate Baroque **town hall** immediately opposite has a two-storey colonnade.

SEAFOOD AND CULTURE

Every morning the **market** next to the cathedral supplies the local residents (and canny tourists) with generous quantities of produce from the sea and the *huerta*.

The **Espai d'Art Contemporani de Castelló** (EACC); Calle Prim, tel: 964 72 35 40; open Tues–Sun 11am–8pm) contributes a distinctly modern feel to this old town. The municipal gallery here is devoted to avant-garde works by Spanish and international artists.

The ★ **Museu de Belles Arts** (open Tues–Sat 10am–8pm, Sun 10am–2pm), just north of Plaza Mayor (Calle Caballeros 25), houses an archaeological collection, countless pieces of traditional pottery from the region and a number of works by Francesc Ribalta (1565–1628).

Ten paintings by Francisco de Zurbarán (1598–1664) are the principal showpieces at the **Convento des las Capuchinas** in the narrow Calle Nuñez de Arce (open daily 4–8pm).

Avenida del Mar leads down from the cathedral to the sea and the harbour quarter about 4km (2½ miles) away, where waiting staff at the *maris-*

querías overlooking the promenade await the arrival of hungry, seafood lovers.

VILAFAMES

From the C-232 towards Lucena del Cid, a side road leads to **Vilafamés**, a medieval mountain village below a red sandstone fortress, where it is surprising to find an interesting collection of contemporary art and sculpture. On display in the ★ **Museo d'Art Contemporani**, housed since 1980 in a Gothic palace, are works by Chillida and Miró (open Tues–Sun 10am–1.30pm, 4–7pm, in summer to 8pm). The views from the castle with its round turret are also worth checking out.

Below: Casino Antiguo, Castelló (see page 110)
Bottom: Vilafamés

BENICASSIM

Like many other towns in the Levant, **Benicàssim** (pop. 12,000) bears the name of its Arab founder. Literally, the name means 'son of the Cassim'. Otherwise, there is very little to remind visitors of the settlement's long history. It is only in the past few years that the town has developed into an important resort with some 25 hotels, the main draw being some excellent, fine-sand beaches (such as Playa Torre San Vicente).

SHORT EXCURSIONS

One worthwhile detour (7km/4 miles) is to the Carmelite monastery of **Desert de les Palmes** (palm wilderness; 1621) in the hinterland. The radio masts at the top of the dark red mountain ridge make for an unattractive backdrop, but at least the region is now under a conservancy order and can offer a magnificent view over Castelló's coastal plain – at a respectable distance from the concrete seaside monsters.

On the return journey, you could stop off at the **monastery distillery** on the outskirts of Benicàssim to sample some *licor carmelitano*.

To the north of Benicàssim, follow the narrow and winding country lane down to the coast (*por*

Map on pages 34–5

la costa). The reward for this short detour is a splendid view out to sea and of the maquis-covered, rocky coast.

ORPESA DEL MAR

Just beyond a curve in the coast road, the new marina and the perfectly-formed, sickle-shaped **Playa de la Concha** at **Orpesa del Mar** (20km/12 miles from Castelló) come into view. While the town did not escape the developers' full-frontal assault on the coastline, Orpesa can still boast an historic 15th-century tower, **Torre del Rey**, built to defend the inhabitants from Berber pirates, and also an old town of tranquil narrow lanes, nestling beneath the ruins of the all-dominating ruins of a Moorish castle.

New-look battlements
The uppermost battlements of the castle at Peníscola were built for a scene from the film *El Cid* (1961), an epic celebrating the hero of the *reconquista (see page 19)*, starring Charlton Heston and Sophia Loren.

For an impression of how the coast once looked, visit the ★ **Prat de Cabanes-Torreblanca Nature Park**. This 1,000-hectare (2,500-acre) area of brackish marshland (under a conservancy order since 1988) is a habitat for such aquatic birds as grey heron, sedge warblers and peewits. Even the threatened European mud turtle can occasionally be found between the reeds and the salt meadows. The walk from **Torreblanca** (15km/ 9 miles north of Orpesa) alongside the sea, over sand and scree as far as Orpesa, takes about four hours. Return to Torreblanca by bus or train.

Torreblanca Nature Park

PENISCOLA

Probably the most attractive town on the Costa del Azahar is ★★ **Peníscola** (pop. 4,500). Like a rock among the breakers, the old town crowns a narrow peninsula that juts out into the sea. It is protected by medieval ramparts and a huge **castle** (13th century) built on the foundations of an Arab fortress.

HOME OF THE PAPAL PRETENDER

The castle's best known resident was the papal pretender Dom Pedro Martínez de Luna, Cardinal of Aragon ('Papa Luna'), who lived in exile here for several years until he died in 1423. The background was the bitter power struggle that divided the Catholic Church at the end of the 14th century. In 1378, the cardinals in Rome chose Urban VI to be their pope. When soon afterwards the election was declared invalid, Clement VII was appointed and he initially chose Avignon in France as his official residence. But because Urban VI was not prepared to give up the office he believed was rightfully his, the scene became set for what was later known as the Great Schism – a 40-year dispute between rival popes with seats in Rome and Avignon concerning who was to be St Peter's successor.

When, after the death of Clement VII, Cardinal Pedro de Luna took over the Avignon papacy as Benedict XIII, the situation became even more confused. Despite the resistance of Rome, the latter continued to hold office, but, in 1411, fearing a violent backlash from Rome, he moved his residence to Peníscola. And in the castle at Peníscola, donated to him by the knights of the Montesa Order, he devoted himself to theological study and continued to wait for the call to come.

But it never did. Instead, the man recognised as Pope Benedict XIII by only a few of the locals spent his life fighting Rome. Branded as a heretic, he survived poison attacks and months of siege. The stubborn Papa Luna died at the age of 95. The

Star Attraction
● Peníscola

*Below and bottom:
scuba divers and
sun bathers, Peníscola*

Map on pages 34–5

abdication in 1429 of his successor Clement VIII ended this unhappy rift within the Church.

THE OLD TOWN AND CASTILLO

Against the uninterrupted phalanx of modern residential and hotel complexes overlooking the coarse-sand of **Playa Norte**, the historic heart of Peníscola now looks almost picturesque, a town in miniature: white, cube-shaped houses, narrow alleyways, floral balconies and windows. If you wish to explore the old town *(casco urbano)*, park your car on the northern promenade.

Worth a visit in Peníscola are the rooms and the 64-m (210-ft) high terrace at the ★ **Castillo** (open daily 9.30am–1pm, 3.15–6pm, summer 10am–2.30pm, 4.30–8.30pm). Cannon redoubts on the town wall provide fine views out to sea; souvenir shops sell crafts and tourist knick-knacks.

Below: San Bartolomeu, Benicarló
Bottom: Vinaròs street

BENICARLO

Originally a Moorish farmstead, **Benicarló** (pop. 20,000) was awarded its port charter during the 14th century by Pedro II of Aragón. Its inhabitants have traditionally earned their living from fishing and farming, but tourism and industry have contributed to the town's recent growth.

The attractive town centre is dominated by the **Iglesia San Bartolomé** (1743), with its Baroque main portal and dome of blue-glazed *azulejos*. The coast road, Avenida Papa Luna, lined by high-rise blocks, links Benicarló with Peníscola.

VINAROS

Vinaròs (pop. 22,500) derives its importance as the port and administrative centre for the Maestrazgo region *(see page 45)*. The promenade, with its lively market hall and the late-Gothic **Asunción** parish church (16th century), are of interest, but it is the town's restaurants that draw in the outsiders. These are noted for their crayfish and prawn dishes, and, as promised by the town's name, good wine and rice are guaranteed.

3: El Maestrazgo

Map
on pages
34–5

Vinaròs – Sant Mateu – Morella – Forcall – Rubielos de Mora – València (355km/220 miles including detour to Teruel)

A little-known world, seemingly a million miles from the holiday resorts beside the coastal motorway, begins just a few kilometres from the Costa del Azahar. Rough tracks snake their way through the starkly beautiful scenery of barren upland plain, with semi-abandoned mountain villages, almost unchanged since the Middle Ages.

The Maestrazgo (Catalan: Maestrat), with its castles, palaces and open landscapes, is reminiscent of the Castilian *meseta*. Teruel, a jewel of Moorish-influenced Mudéjar architecture, is the destination for a detour into Aragón. Allow two to three days for this circular tour.

INTO THE HINTERLAND

Leave **Vinaròs** *(see page 44)* on the N-232, crossing the coastal plain and then climbing into the mountainous hinterland. The prevailing colours are soon no longer the green of the fruit plantations or the blue of the sea, but the grey of the rocks and the brown and ochre of cracked earth. The scenery changes to table-top peaks, monolithic hilltops and steep slopes with sparse growth;

Below: El Maestrazgo landscape
Bottom: La Iglasuela del Cid

Map
on pages
34–5

*Below: Palacio Villores
in Sant Mateu
Bottom: the Santa María
fountain*

in the valleys olives and almonds are cultivated on the terraced fields. The harsh climate in the Maestrazgo is strikingly different to that of the Mediterranean coast. In the winter, bitterly cold west winds whistle over the mountains; in the summer a dry heat persists throughout the day, but at night it is often inhospitably cool.

SANT MATEU

The one-time importance of ★ **Sant Mateu** (pop. 1,800; 5km/3 miles from the N-232), formerly the historic capital of the region, is still evident from the surviving buildings. The central **Plaza Mayor** with its colonnades and globe-shaped **Santa María fountain**, together with the **Palacio Villores** (16th century; Calle València) create a dramatic effect. The facade of the **parish church** (13th century) bears some Romanesque features, although the large nave was built in Gothic style (14th century). There are an impressive four municipal museums in town.

PREHISTORIC CAVE PAINTINGS

About 15km (9 miles) south of Sant Mateu, between the villages of **Tírig** and **Albocácer**, hidden away in the **Barranco de la Valltorta** (Valltorta Gorge), are some impressive, prehis-

toric ★ **cave paintings** (open Wed–Sun 10am–2pm, 4–7pm; tel: 964 76 10 25). Other fine examples of very early artwork can be found in the ★ **Cueva Remigia** (3-km/2-mile long footpath from the road into the Gasulla Gorge) near **Ares del Maestre**, a few kilometres further west along the CS-802. Because of the difficult terrain, it is best to view these rock drawings with a guide.

The rock paintings that have been found in as many as 150 different places in the Levant are thought to be at least 10,000 years old. But some of these Stone Age drawings look remarkably contemporary. The hunter figures in the Cueva de Remigia, for example, are in some respects similar to modern comics and graffiti art.

Armed with spears or bow and arrow, the stylised figures on the rock walls are shown chasing bulls, wild boars or goats. The natural colouring is made from a mixture of iron oxide, dust and blood. An expressionist-style overlay on the legs and upper-body creates an unusual three-dimensional impression of movement.

There has been much speculation about why these figures were painted. Were they to do with invocation of animal spirits, spells or messages to the afterworld? Compared with similar finds in Altamira (near Santander) or Lascaux (in the Dordogne valley), where the paintings are older and more naturalistic in style, the Levantine artists exhibit greater spontaneity – which may explain why so many paintings have been found.

Star Attraction
● Morella

The Montesa Order
The name of the region, El Maestrazgo, derives from *maestre*, the grandmaster of the Montesa Order, which was based in Sant Mateu from the 14th to the 16th centuries. The order's knights saw themselves as the successors to the Templars, who, during the 12/13th century, acted as a kind of Christian militia protecting western pilgrims and the sacred tomb in Jerusalem from non-believers. In the fiercely disputed borderland of Aragón, the Order of Montesa were the ideological and military spearhead of the *reconquista*, and they have left their mark on their native villages in the form of castles and fortress walls.

MORELLA

The town of ★★ **Morella** (pop. 2,700), which has suffered from a dwindling population for decades now, has largely retained its medieval appearance within the 2.5-km (1½-mile) town walls, which date from the 14th century. The rows of houses are clustered around a 1,070-m (3,510-ft) high rock cone crowned by an imposing ruined castle.

Walk from the car park in the northeast of the village and enter the old town through the twin-towered Puerta de San Miguel. The **Museo de Morella** (Plaza de San Miguel) has a collec-

Portal de Sant Mateu, Morella

Map
on pages
34–5

House of the miracle
Pictured in a plaque, on a house in Morella's Calle de la Virgin, is a miracle that St Vincent de Ferrer is said to have performed in 1414 when he stayed here as a guest. With no meat to offer the saint, a housewife decided in desperation to cut up her son for the stew pot. St Vincent brought the boy back to life again – but one little finger was missing: his mother had eaten it when checking the dish for seasoning.

Iglesia Arcipiscopal Santa María la Mayor

tion of fossils found locally and also has a number of dinosaur models.

The adjoining Calle Juan Giner opens on to ★ **Calle Don Blasco d'Alagón** shopping precinct (Sunday market), lined by sturdy arcades. Also worth noting along the road are some beautiful examples of Gothic secular architecture, such as the ★ **Palacio Cardenal Ram** (now a hotel) and the **town hall**. In the west, the arcades open on to Plaza Colón, from where there is a splendid panoramic view over the mountains and the mighty fortress above the town.

SANTA MARIA LA MAYOR

Take the sloping Calle Virgen de Vallivana up to the ★★ **Iglesia Arcipiscopal Santa María la Mayor** (1343), one of the finest Gothic churches in the València region, built on the foundations of a Moorish mosque. The most impressive features of the collegiate church are the two sculptured portals, the ★★ **Puerta de los Apóstoles** and the **Puerta de las Vírgenes**. Inside, a finely carved spiral staircase leads up to the choirloft, where there is a superb organ (18th century).

Among the treasures in the ★ **Museo Eclesiástico** (entrance in the side nave) are Francesc Ribalta's *St Rochus* (16th century), two Gothic altar panels by Joan Reixac, and codices from the 12th–14th centuries (daily 11am–2pm, 4–8pm).

EL CASTILLO

Follow the path from the church up to Plaza de San Francisco and the former ★ **monastery** (1272) of the same name. The demanding climb, with steep bends to the ruined ★★ *castillo*, starts just behind the evocative ruins of the cloisters.

Iberians and Romans had built on the rock before the Moors and the Valencians – in fact the region around Morella was certainly inhabited around 2500BC. One-time masters of the castle include El Cid, the *reconquista* general, Blasco d'Alagón, and the Carlist general, Cabrera, feared as the 'tiger of the Maestrazgo'. In 1838, his troops caught the castle defenders completely by surprise by entering at night through the overhanging closet. The view over the table mountains and terraced fields, particularly from the citadel, is breathtaking (daily 10am–7pm).

Morella is noted for its decorative weavings (rugs and carpets), fossils and aromatic honey.

Star Attractions
● Santa María la Mayor, Morella
● the Castillo, Morella

EXCURSIONS – WALKS FROM MORELLA

Worth a visit if you have time are the **prehistoric rock paintings** near Morella La Vella farmstead (10km/7 miles to the northwest; accessible on only partially metalled track), and the ★ **Ermita de San Antonio** church in a pretty location on a rocky slope. The walk from Morella and back takes about 4 hours.

Near to the village of Zorita del Maestrazgo (16km/10 miles to the north of Morella) is the monastery of ★ **Nuestra Señora de la Balma**. Formerly a place of pilgrimage for the sick or the possessed, it is built into the bare rockface.

FORCALL

★ **Forcall** (pop. 600), one of the region's most delightful villages, has a perfectly-formed ★ **Plaza Mayor**, with compact arcades and majestic 16th-century palaces, such as the ★ **Palau**

Below: Calle Don Blasco de Aragón, Morella
Bottom: a local bar

Map on pages 34–5

Off the beaten track
The best way to explore the rural delights of the Maestrazgo is on the country lanes through the thinly-populated uplands (warning: no petrol stations). Many of the ancient farmsteads *(masías)* were abandoned long ago.

Rural life in Mirambel

dels Osset-Miró, which has been tastefully renovated and is now the town's most exclusive hotel and restaurant.

MEDIEVAL MOUNTAIN VILLAGES

Beyond the idyllic mountain villages of Cinctorres and Portell de Morella and the border with Aragón is the 1,320m (4,330ft) **Puerto de las Cabrillas** pass and ★ **Iglesuela del Cid** (pop. 540). Seemingly unaware of the trapping of modern life, this little *pueblo* dozes on much as it has for years. The town hall *(Casa Villa)* was formerly a Knights Templar castle.

If you wish to continue your journey back in time to the Middle Ages, then take the road to the west for 13km (8 miles) as far as **Cantavieja** (13th-century Romanesque town hall; pretty Plaza Cristo Rey) and on to ★ **Mirambel** (pop. 160; 28km/70 miles from Iglesuela del Cid). In 1981, this walled medieval village was awarded the 'Europa Nostra' cultural heritage award.

The section on towards Teruel leads initially through Mosqueruela, and then over one of the highest mountain passes in Spain, the Puerto de Linares (1,720m/5,643ft; 80km/50 miles from Morella). Branching off to the right is the 9-km (6-mile) long access road to **Valdelinares**, where during the winter lifts carry skiers up the slopes of the Peñarroya (2,019m/6,624ft).

Some 42km (26 miles) beyond Iglesuela del Cid, the scenery opens up. When you reach Linares de Mora, you are in the rural district of Mora, a sheep-farming region with sparse vegetation and a harsh, wet climate.

RUBIELOS DE MORA

The walled town of ★ **Rubielos de Mora** has had a thorough facelift. Of special interest here are the vaulting under the ★ **Portal del Carmen** gate and the old Carmelite monastery, with its two-tier cloisters. Evidence of a lingering sympathy for Spanish fascism can be found on Plaza del Carmen: a polished plaque reminds visitors that General Franco and his troops were billeted here during the 'War of Liberation' in 1938.

TERUEL

Star Attraction
● **Teruel**

★★★ **Teruel** (pop. 30,000), the capital of the province of the same name, is situated on a rocky plateau between two gorges. It is rightly acknowledged as the pinnacle of Mudéjar architecture. Iberians and Romans (218BC) and Arabs (around 800) all occupied the town by the Riu Túria.

Although Alfonso II recaptured Teruel for the Christians in 1171, Moorish potters and ceramic artists were allowed to go about their work unrestricted. Peaceful co-existence between Jews, Christians and Mudéjars (from *mudayyun*: 'the tolerated') lasted until the end of the 15th century, when pogroms and expulsions were carried out in the name of the Inquisition. The Jews fled from Teruel in 1486, and the last mosque closed in 1502.

In 1938, during the Spanish Civil War, Teruel was the scene of some bitter street battles and many fine buildings were destroyed. Most of the town's monuments have been faithfully restored.

Below: Calle Nueva, Teruel
Bottom: Teruel's Torre de San Martín

THE CATHEDRAL

Leave your car on one of the ring roads around the old town and begin the circular tour by the

Map on pages 34–5

Teruel's tragic lovers

The sculpture in alabaster relief by Juan Avalos (20th century), on the tomb of the Lovers of Teruel, captures the heartache of one of Spain's most tragic love stories.

During the 13th century, Diego de Marcilla, the son of an impoverished nobleman, fell in love with Isabel de Segura, whose wealthy parents disapproved of the match, but they gave Diego five years to prove himself and make his fortune.

At the end of this period, Diego returned to Teruel. But he was one day too late. His bride-to-be had already married. Diego died of a broken heart and Isabel, in despair at his death, died the following day.

Iglesia San Pedro, Teruel

★★ **Santa María cathedral**. The splendid ★ **bell tower** with its colourful tiling dates from 1257; the church itself is a Romanesque building to which a roof truss was added at the end of the 13th century. Wood panelling on the ceiling is decorated with beautiful paintings and carvings. The high altar's retable by Frenchman, Gabriel Joli (1538), shows scenes from the life of Mary in Italian Renaissance style. In front of the choir stands an ornate, wrought-iron grille dating from the late 15th century.

Proceed under the cathedral tower to the **Diocesan Museum**, which houses a collection of Gothic sacred art (open Mon–Sat 10am–2pm).

TOWERS AND A LOVERS' TOMB

Calle de los Amantes leads from the cathedral forecourt, past the town hall on the right, and on to the imposing ★★ **Torre de San Martín** (1316). The tower on the town gate to Zaragoza consists, like its almost identical twin, El Salvador (*see below*), of an almost invisible core, around which another tower has been built like a second skin. This principle can also be observed in Almohad towers, such as the Giralda in Seville.

Another Mudéjar-style complex, built in the 14th century and in the same style as the cathedral, can be admired in Calle Hartzembusch: ★ **Iglesia San Pedro**, together with cloisters and bell tower, also has many subtle, ornamental features in Moorish style. Inside, near to Gabriel Joli's altar in the Capilla de los Médicos side chapel, is the ★ **Mausoleo de los Amantes** (the Tomb of the Lovers of Teruel).

MUDEJAR AND ART NOUVEAU

★ **Plaza del Torico** (also known as Plaza Carlos Castel) is the main square in the old town. Here, attractive modern facades contrast with the Mudéjar style. The steep Calle El Salvador leads down to the ★★ **Torre El Salvador** (about 1315). The tiled decoration on this tower is slightly more refined and lavish than that of its neighbour.

Equally close attention to detail, plus some playful features, can be seen on the art nouveau buildings in the parallel ★ **Calle Nueva**.

Returning towards the town centre, the local government and judicial buildings are clustered around the severely classical **Plaza de San Juan**. The terrace for the delightful ★ **Paseo Ovalo** – a popular meeting place in Teruel and not just in the evening – forms the southwestern edge of the old town.

The ★ **Museo Provincial** (Plaza Fray Anselmo Polanco), housed in a 16th-century *palacio*, contains interesting archaeological exhibits and a large ceramics collection (open Tues–Sun 10am–2pm, Tues–Fri 4–7pm). Here you can discover the various methods used to make *azulejos* or glazed tiles. The production of ceramics is still an important local industry.

BACK TO VALENCIA

The road back to the sea (N-234, 160km/100 miles as far as València) takes a straight course through abandoned hamlets and past crumbling farmsteads amid rust-red, iron-rich soil. Occasionally, by the roadside, you will see warehouses, where hams are left to dry in the air. At the **Venta del Aire** service area, motorists can take the opportunity to sample some excellent grilled meat.

Star Attractions
- Santa María Cathedral
- Torre de San Martín
- Torre el Salvador

Below: Museo Provincial,
Bottom: Paseo Ovalo

Map on page 57

4: Alicante (Alacant)

Unlike València, Alicante has always felt closer to the sea than to the *huerta*. This port turns its full face to the open sea, sheltered only by the Santa Bárbara fortress on the bare Benacantil rock. Alicante's soul finds expression on the magnificent, palm-lined Explanada, probably the finest promenade on the Spanish Mediterranean. Both a summer and a winter resort, Alicante's charm lies in the fact that it is intrinsically Spanish with plenty of atmosphere.

HISTORY

Fiery night

On the last night of the *Fogueres de Sant Joan*, Alicante's biggest fiesta, a huge wooden sculpture in the centre of Plaça de l'Ajuntament is set alight by the mayor. As it bursts into flames, the assembled crowd erupts, and the *Nit del Foc* (Night of Fire), when bonfires burn in sequence through the city, has officially begun.

Founded as a trading post by the Greeks, the settlement was expanded by the Carthaginians under the name of Akra Leuke, meaning 'white castle'. Under the Roman Empire, it was known as Lucentum or 'city of light' and by the Moors as Al-Lucant. In 1490 Ferdinand II 'the Catholic', granted the port its municipal charter, and in 1691 a French armada besieged the Santa Bárbara fortress. During the War of the Spanish Succession, the town was briefly captured by Austrian troops.

When Napoleon Bonaparte (1811) took over, Alicante became temporary capital of the region. Its inhabitants were strong Republican supporters during the Spanish Civil War, and in 1936

Explanada de Espanya

supporters of the Popular Front lynched the dictator Primo de Rivera here. Now the city (pop. 277,000) lies at the heart of the Costa Blanca tourist region, and is the most important exporting and fishing port in the Comunitat Valenciana.

Star Attractions
● Explanada de Espanya
● Museo de Arte Siglo XX

SIGHTS

Under the lines of majestic date palms on the ★★ **Explanada de Espanya**, colourful folding chairs and ice-cream stands create a relaxing atmosphere, perfect for a pleasant restful stroll. On Sunday morning, music rings out from the shell-shaped pavilion. The promenade itself is paved with a wave mosaic made from 6 million pebbles. It was completed in 1993.

For a **superb view** over the boulevard and the marina, take the lift to the terrace bar on the 26th floor of the Gran Sol hotel.

Beside this multi-storey block lies the shady **Plaça Portal d'Elx ❶**, with a star-shaped metal sculpture (1978) by local artist, Eusebio Sempere. From the other side of the noisy Rambla de Méndez Núñez, the traffic-free Carrer Major runs past old-fashioned shop window displays up to the central old town area.

A narrow passage to the right (El Portico Consistorial) opens onto the ★ **Plaça de l'Ajuntament ❷**. Two double columns flank the portal of the late-Baroque **town hall** (1701–80). A metal disc on the staircase marks the level against which all heights above sea level are measured in Spain. The Salón Azul (Blue Room), with its mirrored gallery on the first floor, is open to visitors during the week (9am–2pm).

Below: pigeon perch
Bottom: panorama from the Gran Sol hotel's terrace bar

MODERN SPANISH ART

Proceed under the clock tower to the pleasant, palm-shaded Plaça de la Santísima Faç, from where the Carrer Vilavella climbs up to the ★★ **Museo Alicantino de Arte Contemporaneo (MACA) ❸**. This former grain store, built in 1685, now houses an outstanding museum of modern Spanish art, and displays works by its founder,

Map on page 57

Eusebio Sempere (1924–85), as well as by Salvador Dalí, Eduardo Chillida, Joan Miró and Juan Gris (closed for renovation until mid 2004, call tel: 965 14 09 59 for opening hours).

Standing diagonally opposite is the **Iglesia Santa María ❹**, which replaced the main mosque of Al-Lucant in the 14th century. The original Gothic ground plan was extended in the 18th century, when side naves were added and the facade redesigned in Baroque style. It has a richly decorated interior.

Below and bottom: aspects of Barrio Viejo de Santa Cruz

CASTILLO SANTA BARBARA

The tiny colourful dwellings at the foot of the castle hill line the rest of the Carrer Vilavella. At its eastern end, a flight of stairs leads down to the busy promenade. Take the tunnel to the lift up to ★★ **Castillo Santa Bárbara ❺**.

The castle at the top of the 166-m (545-ft) high **Monte Benacantil** dates from Roman times, but was enlarged during the 16th century under Felipe II (open Apr–Sept: daily 10am–8pm; Oct–Mar: daily 9am–7pm).

Sculptures and statues of famous Spanish artists, from Benlliure to Dalí, are exhibited in the **Museo Colección Capa** private collection (open daily 10am–2pm, 4–8pm). The upper section of the castle affords a magnificent panoramic view of the town, stretching as far as the western Castillo de San Fernando, built during the Napoleonic wars.

The ★ **Museo Arqueológico** (Plaza Gómez Ulla, to the north of Castillo Santa Bárbara), housed in a former hospital, displays ceramic artefacts and sculptures from Celto-Iberian times (Tues–Sun 10am–2pm, 4–7pm).

EL BARRIO

Simple houses, delightfully painted and decorated with pot plants, characterise the narrow alleys in the ★ **Barrio Viejo de Santa Cruz**, known as El Barrio, which is clustered around **Plaça del Carme ❻**, making a welcome change to the concrete towers which dominate modern Alicante.

The ★ **San Nicolás de Bari** cathedral ❼ was built in the early 17th century with a rather gloomy Renaissance facade, in what is known in Spanish as Herreran style. Dedicated to the town's patron saint, it has an impressive interior.

ISLA TABARCA

Accessible by boat from Alicante, Santa Pola (the shortest route) or Torrevella, **Isla Tabarca** is 1,500m (4,920ft) long, 450m (1475ft) wide and the only inhabited island in the València autonomous region. Its walled settlement, entered through monumental gateways, was laid out by Carlos III in the 18th century.

The island is popular with snorkellers and sub-aqua divers, and can get crowded. Peace descends after sunset when the day-trippers have gone. Accommodation is limited to a fine hotel in an 18th-century palace, and a less expensive (and impressive) hostel.

Star Attraction
● Castillo Santa Bárbara

Time for lunch...
Around the old town are plenty of bars and restaurants with a convivial atmosphere offering a *menú del día* (menu of the day). If you want to linger over a good meal, it's worth the 10-minute walk to Nou Manolín, near the bullring, which has an excellent cellar (see page 108).

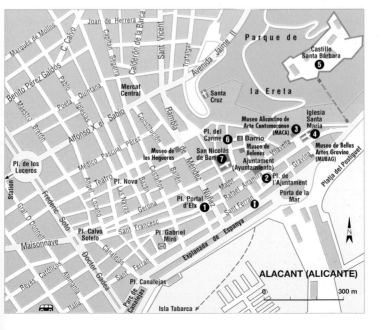

ALACANT (ALICANTE)

300 m

Isla Tabarca

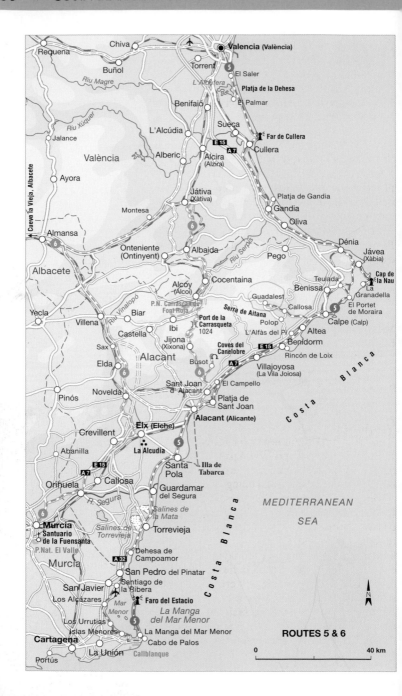

ROUTES 5 & 6

5: ¡Vamos a la Playa!

València – Gandia – Dénia – Xàbia – Calpe (Calp) – Altea – Benidorm – Santa Pola – Guardamar del Segura – Torrevella – Mar Menor (270km/167 miles)

Map opposite

They don't enjoy the best of reputations outside Spain. In fact, the resorts between València and Mar Menor are often held up as the worst examples of how mass tourism can ruin the environment. For those who make this two-to-three-day tour, the reality is actually much more positive.

At the height of the season, the populations of Benidorm, Cullera and La Manga rise tenfold, but despite the invasion, the water and sand stay remarkably clean and the holiday atmosphere is always warm and friendly. It is worth remembering that many Spanish people also like to spend their summer holidays on the Costa Blanca. Visitors who can drag themselves away from the beach will discover something of the region's lively history, sample traditional cooking and take home images of several pretty old towns – none of them very far from the beach.

Strictly for the birds
L'Albufera, the freshwater lagoon nature reserve, is a prime wetland habitat for birds. Its reed beds and marshy islands are home to more than 250 species, including herons and egrets. The visitor's centre can arrange a guided walk for those who are interested.

Benidorm beach

CULLERA

Take the urban motorway from València as far as El Saler, and continue south past **L'Albufera** lagoon *(see page 33),* and a trellis of reed fencing beside rice fields and small orange groves.

The mainly Spanish holiday resort of **Cullera** (pop. 21,000) lies beside a wide sandy bay, bordered to the north by Cabo Cullera lighthouse and to the south by the mouth of the Río Júcar. In between is everything that holidaymakers could ever want for a great beach holiday: bars, fish restaurants, chicken grills, ice-cream parlours, supermarkets and discotheques.

The two pyramid-shaped residential blocks near the beach set new standards in ugliness, and the old fishing village, known as **Barri del Pou**, has little to commend it, but it is worth following the Way of the Cross as it snakes its way up

Map on page 58

the hill to the ruins of the 8th-century Moorish *castillo*, from where there is a fine view.

Many popular fish restaurants (some with live music) are to be found along the promenade.

GANDIA

The town of ★ **Gandia** (pop. 59,000) was once the capital of a duchy ruled by the Borja (Italian: Borgia) dynasty. The historic core of the town is dominated by the magnificent 14th-century ★ **Palacio Ducal de los Borja** (Calle Duc Alfons), once the Borja's family home (open Tues–Sat 10am–2pm, 4–8pm, in summer 5–9pm).

Below: eating out
Bottom: panorama from Castle Hill, Dénia

St Francis Borgia, the 4th Duke of Gandia, viceroy of Catalonia and third general of the Society of Jesus, was born in 1510 in what is now Gandia's Jesuit college. One hundred years later he was canonised. In 1492, Francis's great-grandfather, Rodrigo Borgia, became Pope Alexander VI *(see page 74)*, and his offspring, Cesare and Lucrezia, acquired an unsavoury reputation in Italy for intrigue and treachery. Some rooms dating from the 16 and 17th centuries (the Baroque **Galería Dorada** is especially beautiful) can be viewed as part of a guided tour of the palace.

Also of interest is the neo-classical **town hall** (1778). Adorning Plaça de la Constitució, in front of the *ajuntament*, stands a statue of St Francis,

who founded the old university. Also overlooking the *plaça* is ★ **La Colegiata** church (16th century) with two fine Gothic portals. The former Hospital de Sant Marc (late 14th century; Calle Hospital 18) is now an **Archaeological Museum** with artefacts dating from the Palaeolithic period (open daily 10am–2pm, 4–8pm).

Platja de Gandia (4km/2½ miles) can offer attractive beaches and a wide range of facilities for holidaymakers. The port from where local oranges are exported is worth a visit later in the afternoon when the laden fishing boats return. The catch usually includes red mullet, prawns and crayfish. On weekdays at about 5.15pm in the auction hall, dealers start competing noisily for the best prices.

Oliva (pop. 20,000) is the last town before the provincial border with Alicante. It has no special places of interest apart from a fine-sand beach overlooked by a number of campsites.

DENIA

The town of ★ **Dénia** (pop. 31,000), at the northern end of the Costa Blanca, extends as far as the foot of **Mount Montgó** (753m/2,470ft) and is another place that can trace its roots back thousands of years. Iberians, Greeks, Romans and Arabs all settled here. The name of the town probably derives from a Roman Temple of Diana. Despite the growing importance of tourism for Dénia, the old town clustered around the **castle rock** still radiates a certain charm. Market day is Monday (Plaça Jaume I), plus there's a daily fish market near the port.

If you take a walk through the narrow lanes in the former fishing quarter of ★ **Baix la Mar**, set in an idyllic spot between the fortress and the sea, you will pass attractive cottages, old-fashioned street lamps and rustic-style terraced cafés.

It is worth making the climb to the top of the hill, not just for the great ★ **panoramic view**, but also for the ★ **Museu Archeològic**, where the region's historic past is documented (open daily 10am–1pm, 5–8pm, in winter 3.30–6pm).

> **Vernacular vines**
> Typical of the region around Dénia and Xàbia (La Marina Alta) are the *riu-ráus* or country farmhouses with a vine-covered pergola in front of the door. The muscatel grapes are left to ripen and then sold as raisins.

Below: Baix de Mar, Dénia
Bottom: on display at the Museu Archeològic

Map on page 58

Walks from Dénia
Up **Mount Montgó** (nature reserve): 10km (7 miles), about five hours (quite demanding); from Playa de la Granadella to the old **Castell de la Granadella**: 3km (2 miles), about two hours. The tourist office can provide a leaflet *(Rutas Ecológicas)* with these and other possible routes.

Below: festive Xàbia girl
Bottom: San Bartolomé

The best beaches are to be found to the south of the town by the rocky **Les Rotes** section of coast (there are also naturist beaches here). To the north of Dénia, the water is shallower and the seabed sandier. Try **Platja Les Marines** or **Platja Les Deveses**.

XABIA

Xàbia (pop. 23,000) enjoys an attractive location between the rocky San Antonio and San Martín capes. In between the two are concealed bays such as Granadella, Pope and Ambolo, which during the Middle Ages served as perfect hideaways for pirates and smugglers. Now they are the favoured haunts of sun-worshippers, divers and naturists.

The maze of streets that make up the old town is well worth exploring, and the fortress-like parish church of ★ **San Bartolomé** (15th century) is unmistakably a place of worship – the fortifications were intentional, so that the villagers could seek refuge there when pirates were sighted.

The **Iglesia Santa María de Loreto** also has an unconventional appearance. This concrete construction (1967) was designed to replicate the hull of a fishing boat.

Archaeological finds dating from Phoenician, Iberian and Roman times are on display in the ★ **Museo Arqueológico y Etnográfico** near San Bartolomé church (open daily 10am–1pm, summer also 5–8pm).

SOUTH OF XABIA

A winding but pretty country road leads to ★ **Cap de la Nau** to the south of Xàbia.

There is a fine view out to sea and along the cliffs from the cape itself (where there is a lighthouse and restaurant). The twin community of **Teulada-Moraira** was until 20 years ago just a tiny fishing village, but has been overrun by the tourist trade, and is now mainly holiday apartments. A castle and a fortified tower on the Cap d'Or serve as a powerful reminder of the town's historic past.

CALP AND PENYAL D'IFAC

The literally outstanding attraction of **Calp** (pop. 20,700) is the ★ **Penyal d'Ifac** (Spanish: Calpe and Peñón de Ifach), a huge, craggy outcrop 332m(1,089ft) high perched on a peninsula connected to the island by a sandy isthmus. The old town around the restored Torreó de la Peça tower was a Phoenician trading post. This quarter is now hidden away behind the monotonous promenade of concrete tower blocks and is fighting a losing battle for survival. The most popular bathing beaches are Playa de la Fossa and Arenal-Bol.

Below: Calp and the Penyal d'Ifac
Bottom: dining out at Cap de la Nau

The rock itself, of volcanic origin, is under a conservation order. It is home to some 300 species of plant, and to colonies of birds such as seagulls and peregrine falcons. The **Aula de Naturaleza** at the foot of the **Penyal d'Ifac** is an information centre. A tunnel leads to a staircase, on which sure-footed walkers can climb to the top in about one hour. The summit, of course, affords a magnificent view in all directions.

Boat trips run around the Penyal and into the bays, every day in the summer, from Calp harbour, and several companies offer diving courses.

On the N-332 towards Altea, ★ **Cactuslandia** is a private garden that has been transformed into a riot of colour by over 1.000 different species of cactus and other succulents, tropical fruit trees and a variety of exotic birds.

Map on page 58

Below: Guadalest's bell tower
Bottom: landscape around Guadalest

ALTEA

★★ **Altea** (pop. 15,600) is a genuinely pretty village, despite the recent influx of a number of foreign residents. The elevated ★ **Plaça de la Església** (Virgen del Consuelo church with a blue tiled dome) offers a fine view over the sea, and the silhouetted, towering hotels of Benidorm on the horizon gives a foretaste of the busy resort that lies ahead.

A **craft market** is held on summer evenings in front of the church and a new arts centre has a busy programme of exhibitions and events. **Market day** is Tuesday (on Paseo Marítimo near the marina). The pick of the beaches are **Cap Negret**, **Playa del Albir** (towards Benidorm) and **La Roda**.

EXCURSION INTO THE MOUNTAINS

A popular day trip starts in Altea and heads inland to the town's earlier incarnation, Altea La Vella (2km/1¼ miles), continuing up to **Callosa d'Ensarrià**, a distinctly rural mountain village. In the summer the Sierra de Aitana (1,558m/5,110ft) and the Sierra de Bèrnia (1,129m/3,704ft) present a surprisingly tranquil and cool contrast to the hectic bustle beside the sea.

Branching off from the C-3318 (towards Pego), on the right-hand side about 1.5km (1 mile) after

Callosa, a track leads down to the idyllic ★ **Fonts de l'Algar** waterfall. This is the perfect spot for a memorable picnic.

An alternative route back to the coast is via **Polop** *(castillo)* and **La Nucia**, passing olive and orange groves on the way.

Star Attractions
- Altea
- Guadalest
- Benidorm

GUADALEST

A 15m (50ft) tunnel carved out of the limestone provides access to the tiny fortified village of ★★ **Guadalest** (pop.177), now visited by around 2 million visitors each year. The panoramic view from the *plaza* of terraced fields, imposing sierras and a gleaming green reservoir is unique. La Asunción's white ★ **bell tower**, precariously balanced on the summit of a spectacular rock, is a symbol for Alicante province.

L'Alfàs del Pi, 5km (3 miles) south of Altea, lies amid shady pine forests a little way from the coast. Two-thirds of the 10,000 inhabitants are central or northern European. Local tourism promoters call the region *'el pueblo internacional'*.

BENIDORM

It's now really beginning to show its age, yet people keep coming. ★★ **Benidorm** (pop. 54,000, in summer 350,000) has two long sandy beaches and around 150 hotels, the first dating from the early 1960s. You either love Benidorm or you hate it. Tourist brochures describe it as Spain's 'perfect holiday resort', but for some people it is simply a nightmare. However, if you go on holiday for entertainment, then Benidorm can supply it round-the-clock, seven days a week.

There are one or two nice tapas bars in the 'old town', the only part of Benidorm with proof that it does actually have a past.

The panoramic skyline is best admired from the ★ **Rincón de Loix** viewpoint, a rocky cape above the wide Playa Levante. Integrated into the attractive Parque de la Aigüera in the town centre is a modern amphitheatre designed by the contemporary Barcelona architect Ricard Bofill.

Trips from Benidorm
If you have had enough of Benidorm, try an excursion.
Islote de Benidorm: during the summer months, boats leave from the harbour every 45 minutes between 10am–6pm; there's also a glass-bottomed boat and diving courses.
Limón Express: this panoramic train leaves on Tuesday to Saturday at 9:35am for Gata de Gorgos (near Dénia; basket and guitar making).
Aqualandia (fun swimming pools, etc.) with nearby zoo, dolphin shows; www.aqualandia.net
Cuevas de las Calaveras: grotto near Benidoleig (10km/7 miles northwest of Gata).

Benidorm

Map on page 58

LA VILA JOIOSA

Literally translated, **La Vila Joiosa** (pop. 23,700) means 'happy town'. Drivers may think otherwise, as this town on the N-332 is often a permanent traffic jam. However, the old ★★ **fishing quarter** some distance from the main road, with cube-shaped houses washed in bright colours and enclosed by the ruins of the old town wall, is photogenic. The best local beaches are **Playa Paraís**, **Bol Nou** and **La Caleta**. La Vila Joiosa has a reputation as a 'chocolate town' and has a **Museo de Chocolate** to prove it (open Mon–Fri 9.30am–12.30pm, 5–8.30pm).

Below: La Vila Joiosa
Bottom: Santa Polo

SOUTH OF ALICANTE

Santa Pola (pop. 17,750) has a long history, and there is plenty of evidence for this in the town centre. In Roman times it was the port for Elx and known as Portus Illicitanus. Overlooking **Plaza del Castillo** is the 16th-century fortress, which now houses the **Museo Arqueológico, Pesquero y Acuario**. As well as artefacts from Iberian and Roman times, the museum has displays on the town's fishing industry and other aspects of local history. The remains of a Roman house with a restored floor mosaic can be seen in the **Casa Romana del Palmeral** (Avenida Ramón y Cajal).

Every half-hour, boat trips leave for the offshore **Isla de Tabarca**. The cleanest beaches are to the south, behind La Marina sand dunes.

Guardamar del Segura (pop. 6,500) is situated at the mouth of the Riu Segura around a rocky hill. After the devastating earthquake of 1829, the town was rebuilt away from the castle on flat terrain, but since then it has had to cope with the constant threat posed by shifting sand dunes. To provide some protection, early in the 20th century a pine forest was planted, and this now gives the spacious beaches of Guardamar a special appeal.

TORREVELA

The town of **Torrevela** (pop. 50,200) must surely rank as the worst example anywhere on the

Mediterranean of the destructive power of property developers, desperate to exploit the tourist trade. It has no particular attractions.

There is, however, one unusual footnote to its history, which manifests itself in the annual music festival, held in late July or early August: **Certamen Internacional de Habaneras y Polifonía** (International Contest of 'Habaneras' and Polyphony). Because of the trade in salt, sailors from these parts have close links with Spain's former colonies in the Caribbean, and the town has sought to strengthen these ties by promoting performances of tropical rhythms. Torrevela (Spanish: Torrevieja) forms the linguistic boundary between Valenciano and Castellano.

The best **beaches** are situated close to the *urbanizaciones* of **Cabo Roig**, **Playa Zenia** and **Dehesa de Campoamor** (about 10km/7 miles south of Torrevela).

LAGUNA LA MATA

Before the tourist boom of the 1960s, the main source of income in southern Alicante was salt, and some companies between Santa Pola and Torrevela still exploit the salt flats. Two natural lagoons, **La Mata** and **Torrevella**, have been granted conservation status. The waters provide a perfect habitat for some rare aquatic birds, above

Star Attraction
● fishing quarter, La Vila Joiosa

> **The disco train**
> Night owls can safely leave their car in the garage while on holiday in the Costa Blanca. During the summer months, the trensnochador (tren = train; trasnochar = make it through the night) runs between Alicante and Altea. Starting at 9pm and continuing until 7am, this train stops at all main beaches and discotheques between the two towns.

Santa Pola beach

Map on page 58

Fish specialities

Locals and tourists head to the fishing port of Cabo de Palos for fish restaurants. Specialities include *calderó*, the local fisherman's meal of rice cooked in stock, and fish such as sea bass baked in a salt crust. The high salt and iodine content of the Mar Menor's warm sheltered waters are said to give the fish its flavour.

Los Alcázares

all the pink flamingo. At the visitor centre near Laguna La Mata, biologists organise guided tours and are happy to explain about their research into the ecology of the extraordinary salt marshes. Parque Natural, La Mata, tel: 966 92 04 04.

SAN PEDRO DEL PINATAR

Just across the border with Murcia lies **San Pedro del Pinatar** (pop. 12,700), where there are more salt flats and some of the most popular beaches on the Mediterranean coast (El Mojón, Punta de Algas); you'll also find the inland lake **El Mar Menor** ('The Smaller Sea'), where San Pedro's tourist centre, known as **Lo Pagán**, is situated.

Spanish holidaymakers prefer the smaller resorts on the west bank of the lake. Further along the southbound coast road, just beyond San Pedro, lies **Santiago de la Ribera**, with its beautiful palm-lined promenade and the well-known Club Náutico. As at other places by the Mar Menor, sailing and windsurfing schools, yachting clubs and holiday complexes dominate the scene.

LOS ALCAZARES

At Playa Manzanares in **Los Alcázares** (pop. 3,800), formerly a summer retreat for Moorish kings, wooden bathing platforms, built around the Mar Menor beaches in about 1900, are still visible. The romantic patio in the **spa hotel** *(see page 125)*, unfortunately only accessible during the summer, harks back to quieter times.

As you continue south to **Los Urrutias**, it is possible to get some idea of how the lakeside shoreline looked before the holiday industry took over. A view extends over the reed beds and the Mar Menor as far as the skyline of La Manga.

Outside the summer season, life in the sleepy, old fishing village of **Los Nietos**, now the main beach for holidaymakers from Cartagena, continues at a leisurely pace.

Before turning off to La Manga, it is worth making the detour to **Cabo de Palos**, a headland that juts out into the Mediterranean. The huge lighthouse here was built in 1865, and has for a long time been used as a training centre for lighthouse keepers.

The full name for the chain of charmless concrete towers on the narrow peninsula is **La Manga del Mar Menor** (pop. 5,000). The countless bars, discos and hotels bring the town to life at the height of the season, and few holidaymakers can resist the chance at least once to swim in two seas on the same day.

Star Attraction
● Mar Menor

MAR MENOR

The ★★**Mar Menor**, a saltwater lagoon with an area of 170sq km (65sq miles), is separated from the open sea by a strip of land – only 22km (14 miles) long and no wider than 1500m (about 1 mile) – known as La Manga ('The Sleeve'). Fresh water reaches the inland lake via narrow channels. Man-made cuttings increase the salt content, thereby affecting the lake's eco-system. In summer, the water in the 7-m (22-ft) deep lagoon can be 5°C (9°F) warmer than the Mediterranean, making it very popular with sailors and windsurfers *(see page 114)*.

In the middle of the lake are five small volcanic islands: Isla Mayor, La Perdiguera (boat trips), El Ciervo (road link with La Manga), El Sujeto and La Redondela.

Below: Mar Menor
Bottom: La Manga

6: Through Huerta and Sierra

Alicante – Coves del Canelobre – Xixona – Parque Natural _de Font Roja – Alcoi – Xàtiva – Almansa – Villena –Elche (Elx) – Orihuela – Murcia (277km/171 miles)

The alternative to lounging on the beach is to take off into Costa Blanca's hinterland. In a surprisingly short distance from the coast, there is a wide range of activities available. These include quiet walks in Font Roja Nature Park, studying cultural relics from 3,000 years ago in Xàtiva, Elx and Orihuela, or simply admiring the contrasts between the stark sierras, the fertile *huertas* and the exotic splendour of palm trees planted by the Phoenicians more than 2,000 years ago. There is an opportunity to make an excursion into the neighbouring La Mancha region, the majestic high plateau area of Spain that, since the time of Miguel Cervantes, has been associated with the chivalrous knight Don Quixote and his side-kick Sancho Panza.

This tour is designed to take two or three days, but if after all the hustle and bustle by the coast, you are in the mood for small, family-run hotels with down-to-earth, traditional fare, and a real Spanish flavour, then you might want to make it last even longer.

Below: Villena on the 'Castle Route'
Bottom: Parque Natural de Font Roque

COVES DEL CANELOBRE

Just to the north of Alicante, as you head out towards Alcoi on the N-340, beyond the suburb of Mutxamel (meaning 'lots of honey'), a road branches off to the right towards **Busot**. From here, the way to ★ **Coves del Canelobre** (24km/15 miles from Alicante) is well signposted (open Apr–Sept: daily 10.30am–8.30pm; Oct–Mar: daily 11am–6.30pm). This impressive grotto, where beams of light illuminate the stalactites, is situated at an altitude of 700m (2,300ft) in the Cabeço d'Or mountains.

Below: Coves del Canelobre
Middle: turrón, sweet speciality
Bottom: the Font Roja spring

The caves were formed seven and a half million years ago and discovered by the Arabs in 740AD. Maintaining a constant temperature of 16°C (61°F), the grotto was once used for cold storage, and during the Spanish Civil War it served as an arms depot.

XIXONA

Return to the N-340 and you will soon be in **Xixona** (pop. 8,000), a settlement surrounded by badly eroded sierra. For every Spanish child, this town means only one thing, namely *turrón*, a delicacy produced in many forms but made principally from almonds, honey, sugar and egg white, and usually served at Christmas. The factories in Xixona produce most of this delicious, nougat-style sweet.

To the right, on the edge of the town, is the **Museo del Turrón** (run by the Lobo company), where visitors can make a tour of the factory, sample the different types of *turrón* and buy some to take home (open Mon–Fri 10am–1.30pm, 4–7.30pm; production Sept–Dec).

FONT ROJA NATURE PARK

The N-340 continues northwards over the ★ **Port de la Carrasqueta** (1,024m/3,360ft). About 8km (5 miles) before you reach Alcoi, a country road branches off to the left to the very popular – especially at weekends – ★ **Parque Natural de Font Roja**. In the heart of this reserve, which was

Map on page 58

Popular picnic spot
At Font Roja there are picnic areas among the pines, with benches, barbecue facilities, water and bar/restaurant (closed Monday). There is a choice of signposted walks in the wooded natural park. Avoid Sunday and high season.

Below: approaching Alcoi
Bottom: the church of Santa María

designated as a conservation area in 1987, by the Font Roja spring, stands what was formerly a spa hotel, but is now used as an environmental training centre.

Look out for the unusual *pozos de nieve*, literally snow cellars. These are proof that up here in the sierra it can get extremely cold in the winter. Farmers used them to store ice underground and then sold it on later in nearby markets. Instead of the usual pine forests, the original Mediterranean deciduous woodland – mainly maple, chestnut oak and Valencian oak *(Quercus faginea valentina)* – has survived in Font Roja, especially on the more humid north-facing slopes. In autumn it provides colourful relief from the monotony of evergreen.

Walking enthusiasts should ask at the visitor centre for further information about two good walks: **Barranc d'Infern** (2 hours) or to the summit of **El Menejador** (3 hours).

ALCOI

Before driving on into ★ **Alcoi** (pop. 66,000; 54km/34 miles), turn off the main road to the east and take a look at the prehistoric rock drawings on a fenced-off slope at **La Sarga**.

Alcoi itself is an industrial town where textiles, paper and stuffed olives are produced. It is also known for its sugar-coated almonds *(peladillas)*. The town has an imposing position on a series of rocky terraces, between which five watercourses later converge to form the Riu Serpis.

Worthy of a visit in the old town are the 18th-century church of **Santa María** and the **Museo Arqueológico Municipal** by Plaza San Miguel (some Iberian artefacts; open Mon–Fri 9am–2pm, Sat/Sun 10.30am–1.30pm). Alcoi's **Fiestas de Moros y Cristianos** are famous throughout Spain. St George is said to have saved the town from conquest by the Moors. Ever since, two costumed armies have fought mock battles to commemorate 23 April 1276. The costumes worn for the festival are on display throughout the year at the **Museo Casal de Sant Jordi** (Plaza

San Miguel; open Mon–Fri 11am–1.30pm, 5.30–
7.30pm, Sat/Sun 10.30am–1.30pm).

COCENTAINA

The northern outskirts of Alcoi run seamlessly
into the neighbouring community of **Cocentaina**
(pop. 11,000), where evidence of pre-Roman
human settlement has been found. Rising up
above the town at an altitude of 760m (2,493ft) is
a castle, while the ancient town centre (off the
N-340) is dominated by the vast, square ★ **Palau
Comtal**, built in the 15th century by Count Ximén
Pérez de Cordella, at one time a powerful figure
in the region (currently being restored).

XÀTIVA

The town of ★★ **Xàtiva** (pop. 25,500; 104km/
65 miles) was founded by the Iberians under the
name of Saiti. The Romans called it Saetabis;
the Arabs changed it to Xateba, and it was during their rule that the town enjoyed its cultural
heyday. During the 11th century and for the first
time in Europe, Arab scientists were successfully
making paper here from rice and straw.

Xàtiva later became famous as the 'Borja town'
(see page 60), when, during the 15th century, the
noble Aragonese family settled here (in Castilian,

*Below: Plaça de Trinitat,
Xàtiva*
Bottom: Xàtiva view

the town is called Játavia). This dynasty produced two popes, Calixtus III and Alexander VI, but it was the latter's offspring, Cesare and Lucrezia, who made lasting history when in 1494 they divided up the New World between Castile and Portugal.

MEDIEVAL SPLENDOUR

As Xàtiva has grown little since Moorish times (the population at that time was 35,000) and today has very little industry to speak of, the town centre has retained much of its medieval splendour. At its heart, by Plaça Calixt III, is the **Colegiata de Santa María** church. It dates from 1413, but it was rebuilt in 1596 in a style worthy of a cathedral. The most remarkable feature is the 60-m (200-ft) bell tower.

Opposite the church is the impressive facade of the ★ **Hospital**, with a magnificent portal in Renaissance style. Adjoining it to the west is the narrow Plaça del Mercat – on Tuesday and Friday it is crammed full of market stalls.

The former granary (16th century) by Carrer de la Corretgería is now home to the ★ **Museo del Almudí**, whose prized exhibits are an Arab fountain basin made from pink marble and works by Ribera and Benlliure (open Sat/Sun 10am–2pm, Tues–Fri 10am–2pm, 4–6pm, in summer 9.30am–2.30pm).

Below: Xàtiva's Hospital
Bottom: Museo del Almudí

SPRING

For the Arabs, free-flowing water was visible proof of a town's success and prosperity. Xàtiva is still described as the 'town of 1,000 springs', because many of the old water sources have not stopped flowing. ★ **Fuente de los Veinticinco Caños** (on the *plaça* of the same name, and dating from the 18th century) has 25 waterspouts and is one of the finest examples. Local legend has it that one gulp from each of the spouts entitles you to 25 wishes.

The octagonal ★ **Fuente Gótica** (15th century) on the ornate Plaça Trinitat is equally grand.

Star Attraction
● Xàtiva's castle

THE CASTLE

A trip to the ★★ *castillo*, crowning the towering mountain ridge of the Sierra Vernissa, is a must for all visitors to this part of the region (open Tues–Sun 10am–6pm, in summer 7pm). This is one of the most extensive castles in Spain and access is free.

Situated at about the halfway stage are the Baroque **Ermita de Sant Josep**, the tiny ★ **Sant Feliú** chapel (1262; the oldest church in Xàtiva) and the **Hostería del Montsant** *(see page 126)*, formerly a Moorish palace, but later consecrated as a Christian monastery. Behind the entrance into the fortress is the gun forecourt.

The oldest part of the castle, which goes back to the Celto-Iberians and the Romans, is the **Castillo Menor** (on the west side). The walls and towers of the **Castillo Mayor** a little higher up are better preserved. Its foundations were laid during the 10th century, but the structure that we see today was added during the reign of Felipe V (18th century), who burnt the town down after it sided against him in the War of the Spanish Successsion.

The ★★ **views** from the many *miradores* are simply unbeatable. They extend way over the town and the surrounding *huerta*, as far as the Sierra Mariola and the Sierra Aitana and the seemingly endless plain of La Mancha.

A Little Painter
The painter, Josep de Rivera (1591–1652) came from Xàtiva. It was in Italy where, as 'Lo Spagnoletto' ('the little Spaniard'), he won most acclaim. His home town has honoured him with a memorial on Plaça Espanyoleto.

The castle and Sant Feliu chapel, Xàtiva

Map on page 58

> 👁 **Cave diversions**
> Possible excursions from Almansa include the rock paintings in the **Cueva la Vieja**, near Alpera (12km/7 miles to the northwest; further information from the town hall); or **Chinchilla** (54km/34 miles to the west), with a pretty old town and cave dwellings.

Below: Almansa
Bottom: surrounding landscape

ALMANSA

To the west of Xàtiva, the C-322 crosses the railway line and the Riu Cañoles, before reaching the *autovía* 430 towards Albacete. Passing **Montesa**, a town with strong links to the order of knights of the same name (all that remains now is a ruined castle from the 14th century), you will quickly find yourself climbing Almansa pass (692m/2,270ft) into the autonomous region of Castilla-La Mancha.

★ **Almansa** (pop. 22,000; 55km/34 miles from Xàtiva) is a symbol of the wars which raged during the *reconquista* across the barren border country between Castile and València. Looking as if it grew out of the castle hill, the Arab ★ **fortress** stands imperiously over the town. It is possible to explore inside, but you must obtain the key from the Policía Municipal.

In 1707, Philip V, Duke of Anjou, won a decisive battle outside the town; the War of the Spanish Succession was over, with the spoils going to France. Worth a closer look, in the old village at the foot of the castle hill, are the **Basílica La Asunción**, with a fine Renaissance portal and the early Baroque **Palacio de los Condes de Cirat** (16th century).

ALONG THE CASTLE ROUTE

The *autovía* 330 follows the old trade route that went from central Spain to the province of València and the Levant coast. A number of castles overlook the Riu Vinalopó valley and this stretch is sometimes called the **Ruta de los Castillos**.

VILLENA

★ **Villena** (pop. 31,800; 38km/24 miles south of Almansa) lies beneath the Castillo de Atalaya, a fortress built by the Arabs but extended during the 15th century. The ★ **Museo Arqueológico** in the town hall (Plaza Santiago) is home to an important collection of Bronze Age gold objects, known as the **Tesero de Villena** (open Mon–Fri 10am–2pm, 5–8pm, Sat/Sun 11am–1pm).

BIAR

The town of ★★**Biar**, 7km (4 miles) east of the *autovía*, is the most attractive of these castle towns and a popular place for a day out. Rising above the renovated town centre (with a good collection of pottery shops) is **La Asunción** church (16th century), and above that a 12th-century **castle**. The scene of a particularly hard-fought battle in the *reconquista*, it contains the oldest example of octagonal Almohade vaulting.

During the day, the *castillo* at ★**Sax** (11km/7 miles from Villena), perching like an eagle's nest on top of a 500-m (1,640-ft) high rock, can appear stark and cold in daylight, but against the setting sun it is suddenly transformed into a romantic, picture-book castle. To visit the castle, ask for the key which is kept in the *ayuntamiento*.

NOVELDA

Novelda (pop. 23,800) is one place where saffron from crocuses grown on the plains of La Mancha is processed for use in the paella pans of València. One or two examples of Catalan art nouveau can be seen in the town centre, such as the perfectly preserved **Casa-Museo Modernista** in the Calle Major**,** built in 1903, saved from demolition by a local bank and furnished in period style (open Mon–Fri 9.30–2pm, 4.30–6pm, Sat 11am–2pm).

Star Attraction
● Biar

Below: Biar castle
Bottom: Villena old town

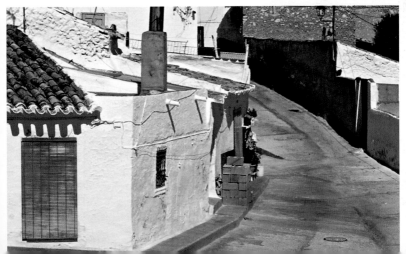

Map on page 58

A fake dame?

In 1995, an American art historian, John Moffitt, subjected the bust of the Dama d'Elx to forensic research. In his book, *The Case of the Lady of Elche*, he argues that the statue is a fake. Even in Spain, sceptics argue that the *Dama* is too well-preserved and does not fit into any stylistic category. Yet the Madrid Academy is convinced that the bust is genuine. What's more, another Iberian bust, 'the goddess of Baza', excavated in the 20th century, has a similar hollow space at the back, probably for storing the ashes of dead kings. How could 19th-century forgers have known about that?

El Huerto del Cura, Elx

And 3km (2 miles) away is the **Santuario de la Magdalena**, which is reminiscent of Gaudí's Sagrada Família in Barcelona.

ELX (ELCHE)

From Novelda, first take the N-325 and then the C-3317 as far as ★ **Elx** (Elche is Castilian; pop. 200,000), formerly Roman Colonia Julia Illici Augusta. Despite its long history, few buildings have survived from then or from Moorish times. Elx is an industrial town specialising in shoes and leather goods.

A LADY OF MYSTERY

What Elx is famous for is the Celto-Iberian Dama d'Elx stone bust, found in 1897 and now in Madrid's archeological museum. Her beauty and inscrutable expression are legendary. The elegant headdress shows her to be a woman of power and standing. The Dama d'Elx, thought to have been carved from limestone by Iberian sculptors around 475 BC, was probably a high priestess, though some experts believe the lady has a dubious past *(see left)*. There is a copy of the statue in the Huerto del Cura *(see opposite)*.

Elx's other claim to fame is a forest of palm trees, the largest of its kind in Europe, with

170,000 date palms *(Phoenix dactylifera)*, which was planted by the Phoenicians and cultivated later by the Arabs. It remains the only productive date plantation in Europe. Located on the edge of one of these plantations is the **Palacio de Altamira**, once part of the Moorish town walls. This building houses the ★**Museu Arqueològic**, whose prized possessions include enchanting Roman statues, such as the headless Venus with dolphin, and a sweetly dreaming Cupid on a lion's skin (Tues–Sun 10am–1pm, Tues–Sat 4–7pm).

The blue-domed Baroque ★**Basílica Santa María** (17th century) is the setting on 14 and 15 August every year for the **Misteri d'Elx**, a unique liturgical drama featuring some spectacular special effects.

Star Attraction
● Orihuela

Below: Basílica Santa María
Bottom: Elx tourist office

PRIVATE GARDEN

Part of the palm forest has been enclosed to form a delightful private garden, the ★**Huerto del Cura** (Priest's Garden). One palm thought to be about 200 years old and known as the **Palma Imperial** has been divided into seven trunks (open daily 9am–6pm, summer 8.30pm). The **Museu d'Art Contemporani** in the old town hall by Plaça Major del Raval keeps works by Miró, Sempere and other modern masters (open Tues–Sat 10am–1pm, 5–8pm, Sun 10am–1pm).

The **Museo Monográfico de L'Alcúdia**, Carretera de Dolores, 2km (1¼ miles) south of Elx, has an interesting collection at the site where the bust of the Dama d'Elx was found in 1897 (open Tues–Sat 10am–2pm, 4–7pm, Sun 10.30am–1.30pm).

ORIHUELA

The former episcopal town of ★★**Orihuela** (pop. 53,500), known in Roman times as Aurariola, is the capital of the second most extensive municipal district of the Land of Valencia. It has a rich architectural heritage, including Romanesque, Gothic and Renaissance style churches, convents and palaces, some of which have been declared national monuments.

Map on page 58

Map on page 58

Best biscuits
If you feel peckish when sightseeing in Orihuela, the nuns at the **Monasterio Santísima Trinidad y Santa Lucía,** at Plaza Santísima Trinidad 6, sell home-made biscuits and puff pastries.

Beside the central Plaza Santiago (the best place to park your car) is the late-Gothic ★ **Iglesia Santiago Apóstol** (1488). Its splendid main portal is adorned with a statue of St Jacob, while inside, the most striking features are the altar made from marble and jasper quartz and Francisco Salzillo's carving of the holy family.

In the rather gloomy rooms of the **Museo de la Reconquista**, diagonally opposite, there is a display of the costumes worn at the **Fiesta de Moros y Cristianos**, which is held here on 17 July (open Mon–Fri 11am–1pm, 5–7pm).

THE CATHEDRAL

Below: tiled seat, Plaza Nueva, Orihuela
Bottom: Palacio del Conde de Pino Hermoso

López Pozas/Ramón y Cajal (pedestrianised zone) leads to the ★ **Catedral de San Salvador**, built in the 14–15th century with one Plateresque and two Gothic portals. Inside the church, two details are of particular note: the beautifully forged choir screen and the silver altarpiece.

Adjoining the cathedral are graceful Romanesque cloisters, moved here from a convent that was damaged in the Civil War. They give access to the **Museo Diocesano**, which contains Velázquez's *The Temptation of St Thomas Aquinas*, and works by Xátiva-born Josep de Riberas (open Mon–Sat 10am–1.30pm, Mon–Fri 4–6.30pm, in the summer 5–7.30pm).

SEATS OF LEARNING

Despite the poor condition of many of the houses, the nearby **Plaza Marqués de Rafal** radiates dignity. A good example of a faithful renovation is the ★ **Palacio del Conde de Pino Hermoso**, which is an appropriate setting for part of the national library.

The ★ **Convento de Santo Domingo** further east was built in the 16th century and later became the university. Now pupils from the secondary school learn amid the magnificent cloisters (one Baroque, the other in Renaissance style) and the *azulejos* in the old refectory (Mon–Fri mornings only; report to the gatehouse).

7: Murcia

The inhabitants of Madrid or Barcelona usually associate the strip of land between València and Andalusia with tomatoes, broad beans and rustic provincialism. Not surprisingly, few tourists venture into the *huerta* capital and university city on the Río Segura.

Those who do are pleasantly surprised. It's not just the friendly ways of the Murcianos, which shape the character of the town, but also the cultural gems such as the Baroque cathedral. It's worth staying a little longer and sampling the culinary delights. Murcia is famous for its gastronomy and hearty, country fare.

History

Founded in 825 by Abd ar-Rahman II as Medina Mursija, the settlement by the Río Segura was initially part of the Caliphate of Córdoba, and later became an independent Arab kingdom. Murcia's early prosperity derives from the irrigation system laid out by Moorish farmers, and also the delicate thread of the silkworm. In 1266, Alfonso X captured the town from the Arabs and merged the region with Castile.

In the War of the Spanish Succession, when Archduke Charles wanted to occupy the town, the

Map on page 82

Below: by the Río Seguro
Bottom: Plaza de las Flores

Map below

City on the Seguro

Murcian defence opened the dykes for the *huerta,* thus putting the Austrians to flight. During the 18th century, the town enjoyed another period of prosperity, during which time many fine Baroque monuments were built. With a population of 350,000, Murcia is now the 10th largest city in Spain. Politically, it has been the capital of the eponymous region since 1982.

SIGHTS

The beautiful riverside ★ **Glorieta de España** public garden, surrounded by the ornate town hall, the **Casa Consistorial ❶** of 1848, and the rear of the late-Baroque **Archbishop's Palace ❷**, is the city's most popular meeting place.

Cross the Calle San Patricio, with the early 20th-century **Edificio Guillamón,** and you will

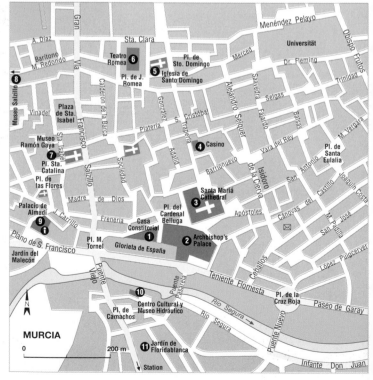

MURCIA

0   200 m

N

soon find yourself on **Plaza del Cardenal Belluga** in the Baroque heart of Murcia.

THE CATHEDRAL

Among the finest pieces the architects of that period created is the main facade of the ★★ **Santa María Cathedral ❸**. Built in 1358 in Gothic style, on the foundations of the *mezquita* (mosque), it was redesigned following a flood (between 1737 and 1792) by the Valencian sculptor, Jaime Bort.

The main actress on the theatrical stage – or at least that is how the extravagant facade appears to the beholder – is the mother of God. Resplendent above the portal is a Coronation of the Virgin scene, while high above it the Virgin's assumption is depicted in the shell-shaped niche. Local saints, bishops and a host of angels play auxiliary and structural roles.

The Gothic **Puerta de los Apóstoles** (1463) on the south side is a replica of the portal bearing the same name at València's cathedral.

An unusual legend surrounds the **Portada de las Cadenas** (1515) on the north side. It is said that an alchemist forged the surrounding chain from stone by means of a secret formula. Because his work was so unique, his eyes were later gouged out so it could not be repeated.

The impressive 92-m (301-ft) high **bell tower** took more than 300 years to build and consequently combines a variety of styles: Florentine Renaissance on the lowest level, Spanish (Plateresque) Renaissance in the middle and Baroque and neo-classical elements at the top. Gothic forms predominate inside the cathedral. The side chapel for the family of the Marqués de Vélez (behind the main choir) has a remarkable star vault.

CATHEDRAL MUSEUM

Housed in the cloister and chapter house is the ★ **cathedral museum** (open daily 10am–1pm, 5–7pm, summer 6–8pm). Among its many treasures

Star Attraction
● Santa María Cathedral

Below: Santa María Cathedral
Bottom: Glorieta de España

are a Roman sarcophagus, a precious monstrance made from Toledan silver, and Francisco Salzillo's *San Jerónimo Penitente* (St Jerome the Penitent).

NORTH THROUGH THE OLD TOWN

Below: Iglesia de Santa Domingo
Bottom: the Casino

The ★ **Casino ❹**, formerly a gentleman's club, is to be found in the pedestrianised **Calle de la Trapería**. Built in the 19th century, it oozes with faded grandeur, the highlights being the *patio árabe,* modelled on the one in Granada's Alhambra , the library with leather armchairs in London club style and the ballroom with crystal chandeliers. If you are here around midday, lunch is very good value. The ladies' cloakroom, with its painted ceiling, is the plushest in town.

The Calle de la Trapería , once Murcia's main street, is well provided with shops, banks, coffee houses and ice-cream parlours. It leads northwards to **Plaza de Santo Domingo** where, every evening, it seems as if half of Murcia gathers for the *paseo* – literally the 'stroll', but more accurately a fashion parade. Formerly the market place, this square is known in local dialect as the *tontódromo* (*tonto* means foolish, vain).

The **Iglesia de Santa Domingo ❺** was built between 1722 and 1745, but very badly damaged during the Spanish Civil War, and only the Renaissance facade has survived in its original

form. An arch links the Jesuit church with the **Palacio de los Almodóvar** (18th century), where two typically Baroque 'wild men' keep guard, but even they have not been able to prevent the arrival of a fast-food restaurant.

Adjoining Plaza de Santa Domingo to the west is an equally attractive plaza, which, like the pink **Teatro Romea ❻**, was named after the local-born actor, Julian Romea (1813–68). Its cafés are especially inviting on sunny mornings.

STARK CONTRASTS

The wide **Gran Vía de Salzillo** separates the old town into two distinct parts. The town planners from the Franco era wreaked havoc on **Plaza de Santa Isabel** and it is now a bleak, concrete desert with car park, while **Plaza Santa Catalina** and the ★ **Museo Ramón Gaya ❼**, devoted to Murcia's painter matador (b. 1910), seem to be almost idyllic by comparison (open Tues–Sat 10am–2pm, 5–8pm, Sun/public holidays 11am–2pm).

On the ★ **Plaza de las Flores**, a *florestería* has been selling flowers by the Iglesia San Pedro for generations. This is one of the best places in town to stop for tapas, and the *pasteles de carne* (meat pies) sold by Bonache, a traditional baker's, are legendary.

MUSEU SALZILLO

A 10-minute walk away to the west is the ★★ **Museo Salzillo ❽**, housed in a round Baroque chapel (Plaza San Agustin 1, open Tues–Sun 9.30am–1pm, 3–6pm, May–Sept, 4–7pm; Sun 11am–1pm). The figures produced by the Baroque wood sculptor, Francisco Salzillo (1701–83), were remarkably lifelike, and many of them now have a life of their own. Every Good Friday, they are taken from the museum and paraded through the streets of Murcia as what are known as *pasos*, or processional sculptures on platforms. No fewer than 26 men are needed to carry the 1,300-kg (1.2-ton) Last Supper figures

Star Attraction
● Museo Salzillo

Artful deception
Francisco Salzillo, the 18th-century wood sculptor, was extremely successful in his lifetime and remains the most popular artist in Murcia. His lifesize processional figures and altarpieces adorn many of the region's churches.

Salzillo's works are traditional, but dramatic and sometimes designed purely for effect. The best examples are the red-haired and grimacing Judas giving the Kiss of Betrayal (*El Beso de Judas*, 1763) and the mourning Mary (*La Dolorosa*, 1756).

When working on the latter, in order to observe genuine desperation, the master played a dreadful trick on his wife. It is said that he shocked her by falsely announcing the death of her own son.

Salzillo sculpture

(La Santa Cena; 1763*)* in the procession, and in addition, the bearers are decorated with products from Murcia's fertile *huerta.* Also on display in the museum is Salzillo's magnificent Nativity scene, with more than 500 figures dressed in 18th-century Murcian costume.

SOUTH OF THE RIVER

Head south and you will quickly find yourself beside the river. In Calle de Verónicas right next to the lively main market, the remains of some of the Moorish walls that were built around the city have recently been uncovered during building work.

Below: Palacio de Almudí
Bottom: Avenida de Canalejas

The compact **Palacio de Almudí ❾**, a grain store built in the 17th century, is now home to the municipal tourist office, and also serves as a cultural centre. Starting on the opposite side of the road is the **Jardín del Malecón**, a park-like promenade.

Situated on the other side of the Punte Viejo (18th century) is the **Centro Cultural y Museo Hidráulico ❿**, where a collection of 24 water mills demonstrates this old, but very effective technology. There is a fine view from the centre's terrace overlooking Murcia's grand riverside facade.

Only a few yards away lie the attractively laid out **Jardín de Floridablanca** municipal gardens **⓫**.

EXCURSION

The ★ **Parque Natural El Valle** (6km/4 miles to the south of Murcia) is a popular weekend destination for the locals, and worth a visit. If you can summon the energy to make the 600m (1,970ft) climb to the top of the **Sierra Cresta del Gallo** (*gallo* means 'coxcomb'), you will be justly rewarded with a magnificent view of the surrounding *huerta.*

You can also look out for a miracle-performing Madonna, the patroness of Murcia, which is worshipped in the **Santuario de la Fuensanta.**

8: Across Murcia Province

Murcia – Archena – Moratalla – Caravaca de la Cruz – Mula – Lorca – Águilas – Cartagena – La Manga del Mar Menor (286km/177 miles)

Map on pages 88–9

Greeks, Carthaginians, Romans and Arabs crossed Murcia on their way to the Costa del Sol, and all left their mark. The diversity of influences, from the Moorish inheritance to Baroque splendour, is a characteristic feature of this region – and one which even Spanish people find unusual.

The relatively small autonomous region of Murcia contains wild sierras and riverside oases, only a short distance from the sandy beaches of the Costa Cálida. Equally unmistakable is the rural charm of the Murcianos; born and bred on the *huertas*, they appreciate good food and good wines. Allow three days for this tour.

Below: Balneario de Archena
Bottom: palm grove near Archena

ARCHENA

Leave Murcia on the N-301 towards the north and Albacete. Beyond Molina de Segura, a road branches off to the left, crosses the Río Segura and continues on to ★ **Archena** (23km/14 miles). About 2km (1¼ miles) from the town centre are the same thermal sulphur and salt baths *(balneario)* at 52°C/125°F that attracted rheumatic

Map below

Map below

Huerta Museum

If you have time to spare, in Alcantarilla about 7km (4½ miles) to the west of Murcia, the **Museo de la Huerta** is worth a visit. Here you can admire the traditional costumes and farmhouses, while an old waterwheel quietly turns (open Tues–Sun 10.30am–6pm).

Valle de Ricote

Romans. Of interest in the **Termas** spa hotel are the Moorish-style rooms (19th century); palm and eucalyptus trees abound in the riverside gardens.

UP THE SEGURA VALLEY

The Río Segura valley as far as Cieza is known as the ★★ **Valle de Ricote**. It remained in Moorish hands for much longer than all other Span-

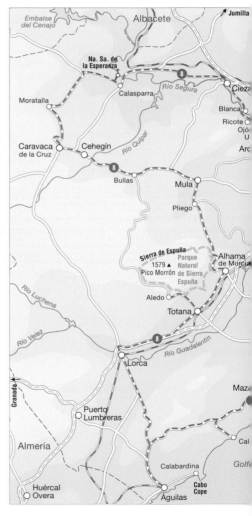

ish regions. In fact, it was 1614 before Felipe III finally took control here. Strangely, even the landscape retains many oriental features. The bare sierra towers above the valley, while magnificent date palms, lemon, peach and apricot orchards thrive on the river plain. Between river and mountain lie the villages of **Ulea**, **Ojós** and **Blanca**.

★ **Ricote**, 2km (1¼ miles) up the mountains above the river, was at one time the fortified

Star Attraction
● **Valle de Ricote**

Below: Ricote
Bottom: statue of St John in Caravaca de la Cruz

ROUTE 8

Map on pages 88–9

capital for the Arab colonists. Of interest here are the parish church and the Baroque **Palacete de Llamas** (18th century). The **Venta del Sordo** (tel: 968 69 71 50) serves delicious local fare.

Wine and Rice Country

One of the best of the Murcia region's full-bodied wines can be sampled in **Jumilla**, to the northeast of Cieza, up on the barren Castilian plain (35km/22 miles from Cieza; family-owned wine museum by appointment only, tel: 968 75 60 64).

Below: grape harvest in Jumilla
Bottom: Caravaca de la Cruz

The best-known grower in the wine town of Jumilla, the **Bodega Bleda** (established 1917; Avenida Yecla 26, tel: 968 78 00 12), produces the rich Castillo Jumilla as well as some notable young wines (sampling and sale by appointment).

Otherwise, if you follow the course of the Segura, after 21km (13 miles) you will come to the town of ★ **Calasparra** (pop. 9,000), the centre of rice growing in Spain, and boasting a protected certificate of origin. The especially fine paella grain is available everywhere in the town.

Moratalla

★ **Moratalla** (pop. 8,900; 19km/12 miles from Calasparra) is the main town in the remote north-

western corner of Murcia. The ancient town centre has changed little over the centuries. Above it towers a **citadel** with a 30-m (100-ft) high tower (Torre de Homenaje), built by the Santiago Order (14th century).

It is almost a pleasure to get lost in the maze of tiny alleyways. The ★ **view** from the church square extends over the valley and the wooded mountainsides. **Pico Revolcadares**, at 2,027m (6,650ft), visible on the western horizon, is the highest mountain in the region.

Star Attractions
● Caravaca de la Cruz
● Santuario de la Santísima y Vera Cruz

CARAVACA DE LA CRUZ

★★ **Caravaca de la Cruz** (pop. 21,000), some 13km (8 miles) to the south, is a town closely associated with the *reconquista*. The double-armed cross *(La Vera Cruz)* is said to have appeared miraculously before the Moorish prince, Abu Said, whereupon he released the priest incarcerated in the *castillo* and converted to Christianity.

The ★★ **Santuario de la Santísima y Vera Cruz** (1617), in the castle, is an impressive shrine devoted to the miracle-performing cross. The church museum contains a display of precious monstrances (open Thur–Sat 10am–1pm, 4–6pm, Sun 11am–2pm).

A ★ **castle**, built in the 15th century by the Knights Templar, is well preserved. According to legend, during a Moorish siege, the parched, defending troops braved one last, desperate sortie in search of water. When they returned with wine instead of water, the fighting men recovered their strength and the attacking forces were forced to surrender. Since then, the **Fiesta de la Vera Cruz**, which commemorates the lifting of the siege, has been celebrated at the beginning of May. The highlight is the Race of the Wine Horses (Caballos del Vino) on the castle hill.

Mountain shrine
About 5km (3 miles) north of Calasparra, hidden in the mountains, is the **Santuario de Nuestra Señora de la Esperanza**, where pilgrims still pay homage to the Madonna (*La Pequeñica*, 'the little one') in a rock chapel.

Santuario de la Santísima y Vera Cruz

ATTRACTIVE OLD TOWN

Caravaca's old town is well worth a tour. Immediately below the Templar castle stands the

Map on pages 88–9

Below and bottom: statue and street scene, Cehegín

impressive ★ **Iglesia El Salvador** (16th century), whose mighty pillars support a Gothic star vault, while on the adjoining Plaza del Arco, overlooked by an 18th-century town hall, statues of *moro* and *cristiano* (1985) feign a peaceful show of harmony.

A 16th-century Carmelite monastery in the narrow Calle Mayor houses a small, ecclesiastical museum, and the town's shop windows are stacked full of souvenir crosses in all sizes and at all prices.

CEHEGIN

Some 7km (4 miles) to the east of Caravaca lies the town of **Cehegín** (pop. 13,000). It is best known for its fruit and almond plantations, plus some marble quarries, but it also has an attractive ★ **old town**.

Of special interest here are the **Ermita de la Concepción** (15th century; timber ceiling in Mudéjar style), the grand **Palacio de los Fajardos** (18th century) and the ★ **Museo Arqueológico**, Plaza de Castillo 1 (open daily 10.30am–1.30pm). Exhibits on display here include finds from the nearby Cueva de la Peña Rubia (Copper and Bronze Age) and also a Visigoth settlement (Ciudad de Begastri).

MULA

Tinned peaches are now almost synonymous with ★ **Mula** (16km/10 miles from Bullas), a little town beneath the ★ **Castillo de los Vélez**, which Luis Fajardo, the first Marqués de los Vélez, built in the 16th century on a rocky needle. The dynasty's burial chapel can be seen in the cathedral at Murcia *(see page 83)*.

It's worth taking a stroll along the Calle del Marqués, in the historic town centre, as far as the main square, where you can pay a visit to the church of **San Miguel** (16th century), and also the Baroque **Palacio de Menahermosa**, which contains an interesting collection of old Iberian art.

SIERRA DE ESPUNA

This route now takes an undulating course along the C-3315, initially past extensive almond plantations, as far as **Pliego**. Thereafter, the desolate foothills of the Sierra de Espuña display a series of dramatic folds until just before you reach **Alhama de Murcia** (29km/18 miles from Mula). It is well worth taking a detour up into the mountains. The 8.5-km (5-mile) climb starts on the right-hand side just beyond the town.

The commanding slopes of ★ **Parque Natural Sierra de Espuña** display a surprising greenness. Only the Pico Morrón (1,579m/5,180ft) has no pine trees; the conifers elsewhere were planted at the end of the 19th century. Another intervention by man was the introduction in 1970 of the Atlas moufflon (a wild sheep) from Morocco. The wide firebreaks in the forest are sign of the constant threat to the woodland.

TOTANA AND ALEDO

Follow the *autovía* 340 along the Río Guadalentin valley. Just to the right of this highway is the little town of **Totana**, noted for its potters and pottery studios. The town centre is pretty.

★ **Aledo** (4km/2½ miles to the north) is dominated by a *castillo*, formerly of great strategic importance as a watchtower over the valley, and

Below: Castillo de los Vélez
Bottom: Mula's rooftops from the Castillo

Map
on pages
88–9

it was fiercely contested for a long time. This small town would make a perfect location for any cloak-and-dagger film. The castle's huge tower was built by the Moors in the 11th century.

LORCA

Below: facade on Lorca's Plaza de España
Bottom: Casa de los Guevara

★★ **Lorca** (pop. 75,000; 33km/21 miles from Alhama) is sometimes known as the Ciudad del Sol – 'the sunshine town', but it's a label that needs to be played down, because the summer heat here is often simply unbearable. During the *reconquista,* Lorca was on the boundary between Moorish Granada and Christian Castile. The huge castle high above the town testifies to the fierce battles of this era.

In the town centre, by the Baroque Plaza de España, stands the monumental trio of **town hall** (Casa Consistorial; 17/18th century), **courthouse** (Palacio del Corregidor) and ★ **Colegiata San Patricio** (16th century; altar paintings by Pedro Camacho). Calle Alamo runs to the left past the town hall to the splendid ★ **Casa de los Guevara**. The eponymous family proclaimed their prosperity with a fantastic Baroque portal (1694; viewings by appointment with the tourist office).

The ★ **Columna Miliaria**, a Roman milestone on Plaza San Vicente, dates from the reign of Emperor Augustus (27BC to AD14).

AGUILAS

Follow the C-3211 for 36km (22 miles), over the coarse grasses growing sparsely on the mountainsides, to return to the sea near **Águilas**. This southernmost resort on the Costa Cálida has always held an appeal for *Murcianos* and *Madrileños*, but is becoming increasingly popular with foreign tourists, who appreciate the many different types of beaches between rocky capes and tiny offshore islands.

The town centre by the harbour consists of Plaza de España, plus fountain and luxuriant, tropical-style park. Steps by the Calle Escaleras lead up to the ★ **Barrio antiguo**, where two defunct windmills have survived intact.

The best *playas* for swimming and snorkelling are to be found towards the eastern Cabo Cope, such as Calabardina and Hornillo.

The sierra to the northeast of Águilas has one of the lowest rainfall counts in the whole of the Iberian peninsula, but the bizarre rocks are not without their charm. After about 31km (19 miles), a narrow road branches off to the coast to the ★ **Puntas de Calnegre**, where wind, sea and sun have created a stony, sharp-edged desert.

Some 53km (33 miles) beyond Águilas lies **Puerto de Mazarrón**, a fishing village and holiday resort, which only comes to life during the summer. The quieter beaches are to the east near Isla Plana and La Azohía.

CARTAGENA

★ **Cartagena** (pop. 176,000), the second largest town in the region, was founded by the Carthaginians in 223BC. The Romans, Byzantines and Arabs all took advantage of the perfect natural harbour, surrounded by mountains rich in ore. The town remains the largest Spanish naval base on the Mediterranean, and barracks, sailors and warships are all part of everyday life here. The best view of the harbour area is from the restored **Castillo de la Concepción**.

The busy Calle Mayor runs from the town hall to Plaza San Sebastián, where it is hard to

Star Attraction
● Lorca

Souvenir hunting
For some well made souvenirs such as pottery and basketware, visit the well-stocked **Centro de Artesanía** in Lorca.

Below: mosaic and chapel
Bottom: Rincon del Homilo, Águilas

Map on pages 88-89

Below: Cartagena facade detail
Bottom: the Casa Maestre
Right: festive dress, Lorca

miss the striking art nouveau facade of the former ★ **Gran Hotel** (1916). The locals could afford such elaborate palaces when the ore mines in the sierra were booming. A similar example is the ★ **Casa Maestre,** by the plane trees on Plaza San Francisco. Just to the west by the Calle del Duque stand the remains of a line of Roman houses.

CENTRAL SITES

The ★ **Palacio Aguirre** (1901) lends glamour to the slightly run-down Plaza de la Merced. Countless bars and pleasant shops line the traffic-free Cuesta Cuatro Santos. Beside Cuesta de la Baronesa stand the crumbling walls of the Santa María cathedral, built in the 13th century on the foundations of a Roman theatre and destroyed during the Spanish Civil War. In this part of the town many layers of Roman and Byzantine sites have been found next to and on top of one another.

The **Museo Arqueológico**, built above a late-Roman necropolis at Calle Ramón y Cajal 45, offers a summary of the excavation work that has taken place (open Tues–Fri 10am–1pm, 4–6pm, Sat–Sun 10am–1pm).

Opposite the naval harbour, the **Museo Nacional de Arqueología Marítima**, has a display of antiquities recovered from the sea-bed (open Tues–Sun 10am–3pm).

MINING AREA

La Unión (pop. 14,000) has suffered from serious unemployment since the closure of the last ore mines in 1992. Only the gestures of the flamenco dancers at the **Festival del Cante de las Minas**, held every August, go anywhere near replicating the travails of the underground workers. If you are interested in discovering more of the history of the rusting towers in the sierra, you should pay a visit to the delightfully presented **Museo Minero** (Plaza Asensio Sáez; Mon–Fri 11am–1.30pm, 5–7.30pm).

Art and Architecture

Numerous expressive **cave paintings** and rock drawings dating from the Stone Age have been discovered, notably near the Ares del Maestre. Works of art from the **Celto-Iberian era** showed unmistakable Celtic and Greek influences. Probably the most famous example from this period is the bust of La Dama d'Elx (around 475BC; *see page 78*). Many remains from the Roman occupation can also be found in this part of Spain, with the amphitheatre in Sagunt and the columns in Cartagena among the highlights.

Opposite: the Morrish Torre del Salvador, Teruel
Below: Roman amphitheatre in Sagunt
Bottom: the portal of Valencia cathedral

ARAB INFLUENCES

Between the 12th and the 15th centuries it was the Arabs who dominated intellectual and commercial life, and Islamic ornamentation became a characteristic feature of Spanish art. Moorish architects mixed together Oriental themes with French Romanesque and Gothic styles.

This blend of East and West became known as the **Mudéjar** style and it can be seen today in the richly ornamented inner courtyards, the horseshoe-shaped arches, vaults and beams with zigzag or floral arabesques, as well as the colourful roof tiles on domes and towers. Many religious buildings in the Levant display such features. Probably the best examples are to be found in the Aragon town of Teruel *(see page 51)*.

GOTHIC AND RENAISSANCE

During the Christian *reconquista* (13th to 14th centuries), French **Gothic** style gained popular acceptance. Towering, monumental buildings asserted the ascendancy of the victorious faith. Even today, churches in València (cathedral, San Martín), Xàtiva (San Felipe) and Orihuela (Santiago) make this intention abundantly clear.

Later on, artists and architects looked increasingly to Italy, drawn by attitudes to ancient forms and the ideal of *humanitas*. During the 15th and 16th centuries, the focal point for this Spanish

Ultra-Baroque style
During the 18th century, many artists took their decorative fantasies to bizarre extremes (e.g. the Rococo facade of the Palau del Marquès de Dos Aigües, València). The name for this ultra-Baroque style, **Churriguerism**, is derived from the Castilian master, José Benito Churriguera (1665–1725). Also typical of this era are the highly realistic scenes produced by the sculptor Francisco Salzillo (1707–83) from Murcia *(see page 85).*

Below: local Baroque at Colegio de Santo Domingo, Orihuela
Bottom: Art Nouveau in Teruel

Renaissance was València, a city that had long-standing trade links with Florence and Naples.

The painter, Francesc Ribalta (1565–1628), and his pupil, Josep de Ribera (1591–1652) epitomise the School of València. De Ribera, often known as *Lo Spagnoletto* ('The Little Spaniard'), worked in Italy, but had a major influence on his fellow countrymen (including Zurbarán and Velázquez) as a result of his mystical light/dark paintings, or *tenebrism*, a style inspired by Caravaggio.

Because of the tendency towards deep piety and playful decorative work, the Spanish Renaissance was often seen as a precursor of **Baroque**. Visitors will encounter this style throughout the Levant today. Examples include the Santa Caterina bell tower in València, the town hall in Alicante, the cathedral in Murcia or the castle chapel in Caravaca de la Cruz. The main characteristics are lavishly ornate facades, which, with their stilted columns and marble garlands, resemble theatrical backdrops. Inside the churches, magnificent sculptures and paintings adorn the altarpiece *(retablo)*.

THE MODERN ERA

The transition to the modern era began with the **Impressionists** who escaped from the unnatural setting of the studio into nature itself. The best-known exponents of this style include Ignacio Pinazo (1849–1916) and Joaquim Sorolla (1863–1923), both from València, and Ramón Gaya (b. 1910) from Murcia.

In the same way that the architects of the Baroque era allowed their imaginations to run riot, Spanish exponents of **Art Nouveau** were equally unrestrained. As a reaction to the strict conservative/classical building styles, the latter constructed banks, residential blocks and railway stations with sweeping lines and elegant ornamentation, in a much more lively and more visually pleasing way. By far the most famous representative was Antoni Gaudí (1852–1926). Although he worked mainly in Barcelona, some handsome examples of the movement have survived in Cartagena and Teruel.

During the 20th century, eastern Spanish art was influenced by artists such as Pablo Picasso, Joan Miró and Salvador Dalí. The Institut Valèncía d'Arte Modern *(see page 32)* is dedicated to the work of Juli Gonzàlez (1876–1942). This Catalan is renowned not just as a metal sculptor involved in **Cubism** but also in **Constructivism**. Eusebio Sempere from Alicante (1924–85) is well known outside Spain for his kinetic art, which explores light and movement.

Modern architecture can be closely studied in València above the riverbed of the diverted Riu Túria. The hugely expensive Ciutat de les Arts i de les Ciènces was masterminded by top architect Santiago Calatrava (b. 1951), and marked València's arrival into the third millennium *(see page 32)*.

Below: Goya in Museu Ramon Gaya, Murcia
Middle: Calatrava bridge, València
Bottom: Palau de la Música, València

Music

The piece entitled *València*, composed by José Padilla (1889–1960) is undoubtedly one of the region's most popular musical works. This brisk but catchy tune in a marching rhythm still accompanies every Valencian fiesta.

Such popular songs in 2/4 or 6/8-beat *(paso doble)* first appeared in the early 20th century, and they remain on the repertoire of the many village and district bands *(bandas de música)*. When the

celebrations start, these bands are always on hand to create the right atmosphere. In many places, they form the nucleus of important social institutions such as local history and youth clubs.

The melancholy of flamenco is celebrated at the *Festival del Cante de las Minas* in La Unión *(see page 96)*. Joaquín Rodrigo (1901–99) from Sagunt acquired a world-wide reputation as a classical composer for his *Concerto de Aranjuez* (1939), which contains strands of national folklore and is still the most-played orchestral work for solo guitar.

Literature

Of the many writers from València and Murcia, two more than any others enjoy an international reputation. In 1460, Joanot Martorell from Gandia *(circa* 1408–68) wrote his chivalric epic entitled *Tirant lo Blanch* (Tirant the White), based on the adventures of the Catalans in the Middle East; on its publication after his death in 1490, Martorell become not only the first important writer in the Catalan language, but also a pioneer of the European novel.

Works by Vicente Blasco Ibáñez (born in València; 1867–1928) became bestsellers during his lifetime. The lawyer and dedicated republican was jailed on a number of occasions for his political

Below: the band plays up
Bottom: Moors and Christians parade, Alcoi

beliefs, and spent some time in exile in France. He was a deputy in the Cortes from 1904 to 1907. His realistic novels, which are heavily influenced by the French writer Emile Zola, are remembered for their intense realism, dramatic force and vivid description of life in València. The basic message is rather tragic and pessimistic. For Ibáñez 'life is a struggle and the struggle is pointless'. Several of his novels have been translated into English, notably *Flor de Mayo* (1895; *Mayflower,* 1921), *La Barraca* (1899; *The Cabin,* 1917), and *Cañas y Barro* (1902; *Reeds and Mud,* 1966).

Festivals

The religious calendar and important lifetime events, such as baptisms and weddings, provide plenty of opportunities for celebrations. Aside from the religious content and the pure fun of it, the social aspect of the fiesta should never be underestimated. Virtually the whole of the village or district takes part in the preparations, including the funding, thus promoting a close sense of community.

There is a fiesta practically everywhere. Every village pays homage to its patron saint or a special statue of the Virgin Mary with the *fiesta patronal.* Pilgrimages, always linked to the veneration of shrines or holy statues, have a long-established tradition in Murcia. Holy Week *(Semana Santa)* is commemorated with solemn processions, with those in Murcia among the most spectacular.

Moros y Cristianos ('Moors and Christians') is the name for the colourful parades (e.g. in Alcoi) in memory of the *reconquista*, when historic battles are played out by amateur actors. The lively 'Burial of the Sardine' *(Entierro de la Sardina)* in Murcia, a celebration to mark the end of Lent, is slightly reminiscent of the theatre of the absurd. The bloodiest form of the fiesta, the bullfight *(corrida de toro)* continues to enjoy great popularity throughout Spain, despite the protests of animal welfare groups. The *Fogueres* in Alicante *(see page 54)* and the famous *Las Fallas* of Valèn- cia *(see pages 28 and 104–5)* are exuberant

Festive dancer, Lorca

festivals that continue for several days, with bonfires and deafening fireworks as the focal points.

FESTIVAL CALENDAR

Below: preparing for Las Fallas
Bottom: procession in full swing

Many festivals do not have fixed dates, so be sure to check the details at the local tourist office.

February/March: Carnival in Águilas and Cartagena.

March: 12 to 19 – *Las Fallas* in València (St Joseph's Fire). Fireworks, processions and the burning of papier-mâché figures

Holy Week: The Good Friday processions in Murcia, Lorca and Cartagena are especially grand. The following week marks the start of the spring festival in Murcia and the famous 'Burial of the Sardine' *(Entierro de la Sardina)*.

April: 22 to 25 – *Moros y Cristianos* in Alcoi, with costumed parades, fireworks and mock battles between Arabs and Christians.

May: First week – *Fiesta de la Vera Cruz* in Caravaca (Murcia), the Race of the Wine Horses or *Caballos del Vino* on the castle hill.

June: 17 to 24 – *Fogueres de Sant Joan* (St John's Night), Alicante, similar to València's *Las Fallas*.

July: Second week – Patron saint's fiesta in Dénia with bull-running on the quay *(Bous a la Mar)*.

August: 1 to 15 – *Cante de las Minas* flamenco festival in La Unión (Murcia). 14–15 – *Misteri d'Elx,* the Assumption of Virgin Mary as a religious play, Elx. The last Wednesday in the month, *La Tomatina* (tomato fight) in Buñol.

September: 1 to 17 – Autumn festival in Murcia with folklore gathering, jazz festival and *Romería de la Virgen de Fuensanta* (pilgrimage).

October: 9 – *Fiesta de San Dionis*, València, celebrating the city's liberation from Moorish rule.

LAS FALLAS

When, on the night of 19–20 March, a fiery glow hangs over València, and the 370 papier-mâché figures are transformed in a matter of minutes into ashes, then the organisers of *Las Fallas* carnival have completed the hardest part of their job. Every area in the city has a committee that meets months beforehand to plan and finance the fiesta. Item number one on their agenda is the creation of the *ninots*, which are burned on the last night.

The custom goes back to the 16th century when carpenters burned puppets with caricatured features. Now it is corrupt politicians, tax officials and other scapegoats who are the subjects for these grotesque, satirical statues. Many of the references will be lost on foreigners, but some erotic details or sideswipes at tourists in sandals and white socks will speak for themselves.

As well as the great fires, there are plenty of other spectacles to enjoy. From 1 March, master pyrotechnicians meet every day at 2pm on Plaça del Ajuntament, where a knowledgeable public greets every successful *mascletà*, the name given to each cacophony of fireworks, with a round of applause. At night, fireworks *(castillos)* illuminate the bed of the Riu Túria, the most spectacular of all being on the *Nit del Foc* (Night of Fire, 18–19 March). It is a little bit quieter on the 17 March during the *Ofrenda de Flores*, when women and girls in costume decorate the facade of the Desamparados church with flowers. *Bandas de música* parade through the old town making sleep impossible. When people's energy starts to wane around sunrise, cannon shots *(despertà* or a 'wake-up call') bring everyone back to life.

Saved from the flames
The *ninots indultats* (papier-mâché figures voted too good to be burnt) of the past 50 years, together with a selection of historic posters and a gallery of former *Fallas* 'beauty queens', can be seen in València's **Museu Fallero** (Plaza de Monteolivete, open Tues–Sat 9.15am–1.30pm, 4.30–7.30pm, Sun 9.15am–1.30pm).

Consigned to the flames

FOOD AND DRINK

TRADITIONAL FARE

The traditional fare of the Levant corresponds perfectly with the way the landscape divides up into coast, *huerta* and mountain. The basic ingredients are fish and seafood, rice and vegetables, meat and chicken. Products from the different parts of the region go into the flat paella pan to make the Valencian rice dish known the world over: shellfish and squid from the sea, peas, beans and rice from the fields, sausage, rabbit, chicken and pork from the mountains. But the culinary diversity of eastern Spain is much more than the famous rice dish, because every town, every region, has its own specialities.

REGIONAL SPECIALITIES

In the province of Castelló, in particular the coastal towns of Vinaròs and Peníscola, crayfish (*langostinos*), Dublin Bay prawns (*cigalas*) and shrimps (*gambas*) are prized delicacies. The traditional, rich seafood stew known as *zarzuela de mariscos*, 'seafood operetta', is worth seeking out. Monkfish soup or *suquet de peix* is a particularly tasty dish. In the nearby Maestrazgo region, roast lamb (*cordero*) is a favourite, often served with truffles or as *tombet* with snails.

In València, the home of paella, restaurants serve countless variations of the famous rice dish: *arròs a banda* (literally: 'rice aside' – rice, fish and potatoes are served separately), *arròs amb fesols i naps* (with green beans and turnips) and *arròs negre* (with squid) are just a few. In Gandia, the paella is served not with rice but with noodles and is known as *fideuà*. El Palmar, surrounded by the rice fields of L'Albufera, is well known for

Left: al fresco at Cap de la Nou

superb *arroces* and the delicious *all i pebre* (eel in pepper sauce grilled over ash logs). Alicante's contribution to the local repertoire is the garlic and oil sauce, *alioli*, which is served with fish or rice dishes.

Fresh fish such as *dorado* (gilthead) or *mero* (grouper) dominate menus by

The detective and his paella

Pepe Carvalho, a private detective in Barcelona, a gourmet and the creation of the popular Spanish writer Manuel Vázquez Montalbán (b. 1939), never misses an opportunity to eat out. On the road after a particularly nasty murder, he succumbs near Dénia to the delights of an *arros a banda*. In Murcia, he simply cannot resist aubergine in béchamel sauce à la Rincón de Pepe. The discerning detective's watchword is 'Drink to remember and eat to forget'. The recipe for an unforgettable Mar y Tierra paella summarised here, comes from Carvalho's Recipes:

To serve 6: 750g rice, half a chicken, half a rabbit, 250g pork ribs, 250g squid, 12 scampi or other king prawns, 1 tomato, 2–3 prepared artichokes, 4 garlic cloves, parsley, saffron, salt, 100ml oil.

Fry the scampi in a hot frying pan and remove from the oil, then cook the quartered artichoke leaves in the same oil and set aside. Add the chicken pieces, rabbit, chopped pork and the squid, cut into rings. Crush the tomato, garlic and parsley using a mortar and pestle and add half of this *picada* to the paella pan with the cooked meat. Pour on 1.5l of boiling water, add the rice and boil vigorously for 10 minutes. Finally flavour with salt and saffron, stirring in the rest of the *picada*. Decorate with artichokes and prawns and cook for a further 10 minutes over a moderate heat. Leave to stand for a short time then serve. Enjoy your meal, or as they say in València: ¡Bon profit!

the coast, but inland, stews always come top of the list. Alcoi, for example, is noted for *borretat* (made with braised fish or meat). To round off the meal, try a sun-ripened orange, some cheese or *turrón*, the almond nougat from Xixona *(see page 71)*.

No visitor to this part of the world should miss a chance to sample *orxata (horchata) de chufa*, a refreshing, milky drink made from tiger nuts.

The best wines, mainly red and rosé, are produced to the west of València around Requena and Utiel. The vineyards around Jumilla produce excellent, full-bodied red and white wines.

Food from **Murcia** enjoys a fine reputation among Spain's gourmets. Vegetarians in particular will feel at home here. Aubergines, broad beans, pinto beans, fennel, Swiss chard and many other types of vegetables are prepared in imaginative ways or combined in stews such as *pisto huertano*. But meat-eaters need not feel left out. Specialities include grilled kid *(cabrito)*, partridge *(perdiz)* and rabbit with garlic *(conejo con ajo)*. The tasty range of charcuterie includes pepper sausage, black sausage and dry sausage. *Pastel murciano* (a puff pastry pie with a meat and vegetable filling) makes an ideal mid-morning or lunchtime snack. *Hueva de mújol* (mullet roe) is associated with the Mar Menor, *caldero*, a very popular fish and rice dish, is made with various types of fish and served with *alioli*.

> **Meal times**
> The multi-course main meal is lunch *(comida)*, although it is unlikely to be served before 2pm. There is always time before supper *(cena; 9–11pm)* for a glass of wine or a snack *(merienda)*, but if you don't want to eat that late, you will always find a bar with a generous selection of appetisers *(tapas)*.

Desserts include *yemas de Caravaca* (sugar and egg yolk in caramel), *flan* (crème caramel) or *paparajote*, a blend of flour, eggs, cinnamon, sugar and grated lemon peel.

Restaurant selection

Here are suggestions for the main destinations in this guide, which are listed alphabetically after the three main cities. €€€ means expensive, €€ moderate, and € inexpensive.

València

Alghero, Burriana 52, tel: 963 33 35 79. Excellent Valencian and Catalan cuisine. €€.
Eladio, Chiva 40, tel: 963 84 22 44. First-rate Valencian and international cuisine. €€€.
Marisquería Civera, Lérida 11, tel: 963 47 59 17. Well-known fish restaurant. Good tapas at the bar. €€.
La Vita é Bella, En Llop 4, tel: 963 52 21 31. Outstanding Italian restaurant with great family atmosphere. €€.

Alicante

El Bocaíto, Isabel la Católica 22, tel: 965 92 26 30. Excellent tapas and down-to-earth meals. €€.
Nou Manolín, Villegas 3, tel: 965 20 03 68. Sophisticated, local specialities. €€.
Piripi, Oscar Esplá 30, tel: 965 22 79 40. Stylish tapas or fine seafood and paella dishes. €€€.
Restaurante Mixto Vegetariano, Plaza de Santa Maria 2. A rare vegetarian restaurant on this carnivorous costa. Inexpensive and good. €.

Murcia

Hispano, Radio Murcia 3, tel: 968 21 61 52. Classic *huerta* dishes. €€.
Paco Pepe, Madre de Dios 14, tel: 968 21 95 87. Fish and meat dishes. €€.
Raimundo Gonzalés, Plaza Raimundo

Gonzáles 5, tel: 968 21 23 77. Excellent vegetable and fish dishes. €€.
Rincón de Pepe, Apóstoles 34, tel: 968 21 22 39. The place for sophisticated *huerta* cooking. €€€.

Aguilas
Las Brisas, Expl. del Puerto, tel: 968 41 00 27. Good fish restaurant. €€.

Alcoi
Els Frares, Avenida País Valencià 20, Quatretondeta, tel: 965 51 12 34. Just south-east of town, this English-run restaurant (and hotel) is excellent. Good for vegetarians. €€.

Almansa
Mesón de Pincelín, Las Norias 10, tel: 967 34 00 07. Down-to-earth fare. Local specialities. €€.

Altea
Miramar, La Mar 1, tel: 965 84 04 35. Nice tapas bar by the marina. €€.
El Negro, Santa Bárbara 4, tel: 965 84 18 26. Whitewashed, old-town house; fish and meat from the barbecue. Magnificent view from the terrace. €€.

Benicarló
El Cortijo, Avenida Méndez Núñez 85, tel: 964 47 00 75. Fish and seafood of superior quality. €€.

Rosi, Peníscola 6, tel: 964 47 00 32. Basic fish restaurant; inexpensive. €.

Benidorm
Marisquería Naútico, Paseo Colón, tel: 965 85 54 25. Smart restaurant overlooking the harbour specialising in quality seafood dishes. €€.
La Palmera, Avenida Dr. Severo Ochoa 48, tel: 965 85 32 82. Popular, specialising in rice dishes. €€.
Rayts, San Vicente 2. Benidorm's oldest (and best) fish and chip shop for poor deprived Brits. €.
Tiffany's, Avenida Mediterráneo 51, tel: 965 85 44 68. International and Spanish fare with piano accompaniment. €€€.

Cabo de Palos
Miramar, Pasco de la Barra 14, tel: 968 56 30 33. Regional fare. €€.
El Mosqui, Subida al Faro 50, tel: 968 56 45 63. The best *caldero* on the cape. €€.

Calp
La Cambra, Delfín, Edificio Damara II, tel: 965 83 06 05. Basque and regional cuisine specialising in rice dishes. €€.

Café in Plaza Santa Clara,
Castelló

Casa Rolando, Doctor Fleming, tel: 965 83 10 52. German owned with a good choice of fish and game dishes. €€.

Los Zapatos, Santa María 7, tel: 965 83 15 07. Spanish and international cuisine. Very popular with long-stay guests from northern Europe. €€.

Cantavieja

Buj, Avenida Maestrazgo 6, tel: 964 18 50 33. Excellent, creative cooking with an elegant touch – a surprise, given its provincial location. Lunchtime only. Reservation essential. €€.

Caravaca de la Cruz

Los Viñales, Avenida Juan Carlos I 41, tel: 968 70 84 58. Local specialities. €€.

Cartagena

Los Churrascos, Avenida Filipinas 13, El Algar (15km/9 miles north of Cartagena), tel: 968 13 61 44. Definitely worth the drive. The best there is in fish and meat; not too expensive, with a good wine cellar. €€.

Mare Nostrum, Paseo Alfonso XIII, tel: 968 52 21 31. Nothing but fish and seafood. Great view of the town. €€.

A tapas bar in Murcia

Castelló

Casino Antiguo, Puerta del Sol 1, tel: 964 22 28 64. Worth a visit, if only for the art nouveau cinema. €€.

Tasco del Puerto, Avenida del Puerto 13, El Grao, tel: 964 28 44 81. Classic fish restaurant. €€.

Cehegín

Sol, Mayor 17, tel: 968 74 00 64. Traditional restaurant serving local specialities. €€.

Cocentaina

L'Escaleta, Subida Estación Norte 205, tel: 965 59 21 00. Seductive Basque cuisine. €€.

Cullera

Casa Salvador, L'Estany de Cullera, tel: 961 72 01 36. Valencian specialities by a natural lagoon. €€.

Les Mouettes, Subida al Castillo, tel: 961 72 00 10. Nice position above the village. French/Spanish cuisine. €€€.

Many other popular fish restaurants (some with live music) are located beside the promenade.

Dénia

Asador del Puerto, Plaza de Raset 10–11, tel: 966 42 34 82. A fine restaurant for meat and fish. Suckling pig is a speciality. €€.

Gavila, Marqués de Campos 55, tel: 965 78 10 66. Dénia's classic restaurant; it's more than 100 years old. *Arròs à banda* is recommended. €€.

El Raset, Bellavista 7, tel: 965 78 50 40. Great location by the fishing harbour. €€.

Elx

La Finca, Ptda. Perleta 1-7, tel: 965 45 60 07. Elegant setting, Mediterranean fare. €€€.

Mesón El Granaino, José M. Buch 40, tel: 966 66 40 80. Traditional restaurant with a good tapas bar. €€.

La Tartana, Nou de San Antonio 17, tel: 965 42 57 87. Traditional cuisine in attractive rustic style restaurant. €€.

Forcall

Mesón de la Vila, Plaza Mayor 8, tel: 964 17 11 25. Down-to-earth, regional fare. €€.

Gandia

Gamba, Carretera Nazaret–Oliva, Playa de Gandia, tel: 962 84 13 10. Go-ahead fish restaurant with a terrace. €€€.

Kayuko, Asturias 23, tel: 962 84 01 37.Tasty and imaginative seafood and fish dishes. €€.

Many other restaurants along the 2.5-km (1½-mile) Passeig Marítim.

La Malvarossa

Las Arenas and **La Pepica** serve day-trippers paella at reasonable prices. €.

L'Estimat, Avenida Neptuno 16, tel: 963 71 36 33. One of the best fish restaurants on the harbour. €€.

La Manga del Mar Menor

Borsalino, Edificio Babilonia, tel: 968 56 31 30. International cuisine but with a French influence. €€€.

Loro Verde, Plaza Bohemia, tel: 968 14 02 93. Friendly bar, decent tapas. €€.

El Velero de los Churrascos, Edificio Snipe, tel: 968 14 05 07. A branch of the popular 'Los Churrascos' in El Algar; regional fare. €€.

La Vila Joiosa

Hogar del Pescador, Avenida País Valencià 33, tel: 965 89 00 21. Fish and seafood; what else is there? €€.

Lorca

Cándido, Santo Domingo 13, tel: 968 46 69 07. Traditional cooking. A popular spot. €€.

Mirambel

Hostal Guimera, Agustín Pastor 10, tel: 964 17 82 69. Small restaurant with rooms; regional cuisine. €€.

Morella

Casa Roque, Cuesta San Juan 1, tel: 964 16 03 36. In gracious 17th-century mansion. Go for the menú degustación with its typical *morellana* dishes. €€.

Vinatea, Blasco Alagón 17, tel: 964 16 07 44. Regional cuisine. €€.

Mula

Venta La Magdalena, tel: 968 66 05 68. Restaurant by the Baños de Mula medicinal spring, 5km (3 miles) east of Mula. €€.

Orihuela

Casa Corro, Palmeral de San Antón, tel: 965 30 29 63. On the edge of town. Also a hotel. Down-to-earth fare. €€.

Orpesa del Mar

Torre del Rey, Paseo Marítimo 27. Fast food and good fish tapas. €€.

Peníscola

Altamira, Príncipe 3, tel: 964 48 00 38. Old town restaurant in a good location. €€.

Casa Jaime, Avenida Papa Luna 5, tel: 964 48 00 30. Very popular. Rice

dishes predominate. €€.
Txalupa, Avenida Papa Luna 100, tel:
964 48 11 90. Basque cuisine, fine
fish. €€.

Puerto de Mazarrón
Virgen del Mar, Paseo Marítimo, tel:
968 59 50 57. Terrace by the sea. Fish
and seafood. €€.

Nightlife

Discos and Spanish-style pubs (young people's bars with music) get going around midnight, and some stay open until breakfast time. Drinks are pricey, but spirit measures are generous. In addition, some discos charge an entrance fee at weekends. Bars are generally open from breakfast time until the early hours in the morning. During the summer, the busiest nightspots on the coast are Alicante, Benidorm and Torrevieja. The latter two come alive only at weekends in winter.

In Alicante, Eclipse and Fitty are the two main discos; Z is popular with the under-25s. For a more native flavour, go to the old town near the cathedral, where the bars are concentrated. El Caribe (General Primo de Rivera 14) is a Latin bar with free salsa classes. Stylish Desafinado (off the Rambla) has good jazz, and there are many young people's clubs in Calle San Fernando. Doña Pepa, by the town hall, is a classic dance hall.

In Benidorm, the old pedestrian quarter has many bars and cafés. Eros (Calle de la Santa Faz), is a small, supposedly gay bar with a mixed clientele. The main central disco is Black Sunset (Calle Esperanto s/n). Just out of town on the N332 is Ku (open summer only), a 'spaceship' with bars, disco and swimming pool. Right next door is Racha, a similarly big bad disco which gets going late.

The streets around Torrevieja's port are filled with cafés, ice-cream parlours, bars and clubs. Classic bars include the Casino in the port, the Casablanca and Maria Sarmiento.

Sagunt
L'Armeler, Subida del Castillo 44,
tel: 962 66 43 82. Nice location, on the
edge of the Jewish quarter. French-
inspired. €€.

Sant Mateu
Montesa, Constitución 21, tel: 964 41
66 48. Part of a modern new hotel,
specialising in traditional fish and
meat dishes. €€.

Santa Pola
Batiste, Avenida Pérez Ojeda (by the
harbour), tel: 965 41 14 85. Valencian
seafood specialities. €€.

San Pedro del Pinatar
Venezuela, Pescadería, Lo Pagán, tel:
968 18 15 15. Excellent fish. €€.

Teruel
Ambeles, Ronda Ambeles 6, tel: 978
61 08 06. Hearty Aragon/Castilian
cooking. €€.

Vinaròs
Casa Pocho, Sant Gregori 49, tel: 964
45 10 95. *Marisquería*. €€.
El Langostino de Oro, San Francisco
31, tel: 964 45 12 04. Crustaceans
cooked in classic Valencian style. €€.
Vinya d'Alòs, Paseo Blasco Ibañez 13,
tel: 964 45 49 62. Seafront restaurant
with delicious fish and rice dishes. €€.

Xàbia
El Negresco, Carretera Cap de la Nau
3km (2 miles), tel: 966 46 05 52.
French and international cuisine. €€€.
El Nilo, Libertad Bloque 2, tel: 965 79
36 48. Tasty Middle-Eastern fare, like
falafel and *shawerma*, to eat in or take
away. €.

Xàtiva
Casa La Abuela, Reina 17, tel: 962
28 10 85. Straightforward Valencian
cooking. €€.

ACTIVE HOLIDAYS

HIKING AND HILLWALKING

As the trend towards active holidays grows, the number of footpaths in Spain is increasing. Two long-distance routes *(senderos de gran recorrido)*, numbered GR-7 and GR-10, cross the València region, and then there are a number of shorter routes *(pequeño recorrido)*.

The abandoned railway from Caravaca de la Cruz to Baños de Mula (45km/28 miles) has been converted into the **Vía Verde del Noroeste**, which tracks through the Murcian hinterland. Further information is available from the tourist office in Caravaca de la Cruz, Monjas 17, tel: 968 70 24 24. There's also a detailed guide book *La Vía Verde hacia El Noroeste* available at most good bookshops.

A good place to start a walking holiday is in the Sierra Mariola (Font Roja Nature Park; *see page 71*), in the Maestrazgo or in northern Murcia (Sierra de Espuña, Sierra de la Muela). Xàbia is also a good starting point for day trips. A popular excursion from here is the climb to the summit of Mount Montgó. Allow five to six hours for the 753-m (2,470-ft) ascent. If you contact the Agència Valenciana del Turisme *(see page 118 for address)*, they will supply you with a leaflet entitled *Turismo de Interior*, which, together with a collection of loose-leaf maps, offers some useful tips and suggestions. Detailed walking maps are available from local bookshops. If you intend to undertake more challenging walks or to go climbing, it is advisable to contact one of the local guides.

If you want to go off the beaten track, remember that you may well stray on to private land and could suddenly find yourself coming face to face with grazing animals, such as bulls! Look out for wooden planks arranged crossways, which generally mean keep out.

GOLF

The province of València boasts no fewer than 20 golf courses, where guests can play upon payment of a green fee. A full listing of the available golf courses appears in the ITVA brochure entitled *Golf* (available from tourist offices). The luxury Hyatt Regency La Manga Hotel in Murcia

La Manga Golf Club,
Murcia

(see page 124) has three excellent 18-hole courses.

Cycling

The Spanish have always been cycling mad – it wasn't Miguel Induraín's fifth Tour de France victory that started the craze. Racing bikes, mountain bikes and ordinary push-bikes are available for hire in most holiday resorts.

Surfing and Sailing

Nearly all coastal resorts have a *Club Náutico* (usually linked to a sailing club). The shallow and wind-assured waters of the Mar Menor are favoured race venues for sailors and windsurfers of all categories. For further information contact Puerto Deportivo 'Mar Menor', Los Urrutias, (tel/fax: 968 13 44 38) or Manga-Surf, Mar Menor (tel: 968 14 53 31).

Diving

The Mediterranean cannot compare with the Caribbean when it comes to underwater visibility and diversity, but there are still a number of interesting places to dive, mainly along the Murcian coast at Cabo de Palos (with the offshore Islas Hormigas) or near Águilas (Isla del Fraile). However, always be on your guard for dangerous currents. You can obtain further information from Club Islas Hormigas at Cabo de Palos (tel/fax: 968 14 55 30) or due west in Torrevieja at Scuba-tribe (tel: 966 71 99 36).

Fun for the Children

If you are on holiday with children, then you may need to look for attractions away from the beach. During the summer, the 'aquaparks', with giant water slides, rides and fun swimming pools attract thousands of families.

The main sites are:

Aquapark Torrevieja, La Hoya Grande (tel: 965 71 58 90).

Aqualandia, Benidorm (tel: 965 86 01 00).

Oceanpark, Playa San Juan, Alicante (tel: 965 65 24 99).

Day tickets are available, and children pay about half price. All the aquaparks are run on environmentally sound lines, using a water recirculation system.

Giant Playground

Families with children sightseeing in València will definitely appreciate the opportunities provided by **Parque Gulliver**, and really should include it in their itinerary. This popular children's playground, situated not far from the Palau de la Música, is a giant laid out on the ground, but with plenty of places to climb and hide.

Wildlife Park Shows

Many visitors are drawn to the big game, reptile and dolphin shows that are staged in wildlife parks, such as **Safaripark Vergel**, on the Carretera València-Alicante (Vergel-Pego exit; tel: 965 75 02 85), **Río Safari** on the Elx-Santa Pola Carretera (tel: 966 63 82 88) and **MundoMar**, next to Aqualandia, Benidorm (tel: 965 86 91 01).

Tierra Mítica theme park

A giant theme park in Disneyland style is located near Benidorm. Visitors to Tierra Mitica ('The Land of Myth') can explore and experience aspects of the past, present and future of Mediterranean civilisations – Egypt, Greece, Rome, Iberia and The Islands. The spectacular park on the slopes of Sierra Cortina overlooks the bay area. Open all year (until midnight mid-June to mid-September), its amusements, shows and sophisticated computerised virtual tours have proved hugely popular with children and adults alike.

How to get there: exit 65A on the A-7 motorway (5km/3miles beyond the Benidorm exit).

PRACTICAL INFORMATION

Getting There

BY AIR

There are scheduled flights to Valèn-cia. The national carrier is Iberia, tel: 0845 601 2854; www.iberia.com Compa-nies that operate flights from the UK to Alicante include British Midland (tel: 0870 607 0555; www.flybmi.com); Monarch (tel: 01582 400 000; www.monarch-airlines.com); and Easyjet (tel: 0870 600 000; www.easyjet.com). Ryanair (tel: 0871 246 0000; www.ryanair.com) now operates direct flights to Murcia. Scan the newspapers for low-cost charter flights, especially in summer.

BY CAR

Although it is a long way, getting to eastern Spain by car is relatively straightforward, as it is now possible to travel all the way by motorway. From Calais, take the motorway to Paris, and then continue south through the Rhône valley; follow the Mediter-ranean coast through to Spain and down to Alicante via *Autopista 7*. Tolls are payable for motorways in France and Spain. There are Motorail services to Narbonne.

Emergency breakdown service in Spain: tel: 915 93 33 33. Check before you leave home whether your motor-ing organisation has a reciprocal agreement with its Spanish counter-part: Real Automovil Club de España (RACE), tel: 915 94 74 00.

BY RAIL

A popular route is London–Paris–Barcelona, then by Euromed to Valen-cia (under 3 hours) or Alicante (under 5 hours). For details and reservations contact Eurostar, tel: 08702 649 899; www.eurostar.com There is a 20 percent saving on return tickets. Holders of Interrail or Eurodomino passes (avail-able at main rail stations or any travel agent; you must have been a resident in Europe for the previous six months) qualify for big discounts.

Rail tickets to Spain can also be purchased from Rail Europe, 179 Pic-cadilly, London, tel: 08705 848 848; www.raileurope.co.uk

BY COACH

Although it is a gruelling journey, the coach to València/Alicante/Murcia and other Costa Blanca destinations is

*On the road,
between Ricote and Cieza*

considerably cheaper than the train. Eurolines operates sheduled services throughout Europe. There are twice-weekly services from London's Victoria Coach Station. Eurolines (now operated by National Express), tel: 08705 80 80 80; www.eurolines.co.uk

Getting Around

BY HIRE CAR

All the main international car hire firms, and many smaller local companies, have branches in the towns and holiday resorts. It is worth making a price comparison. In the high season it is best to book in advance. Many airline operators offer fly-drive packages.

Car driver's checklist
Drivers need to carry their national driving licence, vehicle registration documents and a Green Card. Third-party insurance is compulsory in Spain: your insurance company will supply a Green Card and a bail bond – essential in the event of an accident.

TRAFFIC REGULATIONS

The speed limit in urban areas is 50kmph (31mph), out of town 90kmph (56mph), on two-lane highways 100kmph (62mph) and on motorways 120kmph (74mph). On-the-spot payment of fines is compulsory.

Seatbelts must be worn by drivers and front seat passengers, and by rear passengers if belts are fitted. The blood alcohol limit for drivers is 0.5g per 1,000cu cm. Drivers must not use mobile phones while at the wheel; and towing by private cars is not allowed. Drivers wishing to turn left are often directed to a spur on the right-hand lane before crossing the road. The police tow away any illegally parked vehicles. In towns the

Policía Municipal deal with accidents; elsewhere, it is the Guardia Civil de Tráfico.

BY BUS AND TRAIN

The Spanish railway network (RENFE) runs efficient services over a dense network – and fares are cheap. A high-speed train, *Alaris*, operates between València and Madrid (3½ hours). The yellow and white carriages of the Generalitat Valenciana shuttle between Dénia and Alicante along narrow-gauge track, and private bus operators serve nearly all the towns and villages.

GETTING AROUND TOWN

A good urban bus service operates in València, Alicante and Murcia. Taxi journeys are charged by the meter and fares are relatively cheap. València has a Metro system with five lines in operation.

CONNECTIONS
València
By air
Manises (8km/5 miles to the west; taxis, bus). Barcelona, Madrid, Balearics; international connections. For information, tel: 961 59 85 00.
By rail
Estació del Nord, Xàtiva 24, tel: 902 24 02 02; www.emtvalencia.es Alicante, Barcelona, Madrid. For information on local routes contact RENFE (tel: 902 24 02 02; www.renfe.es).
By bus
Avenida Menéndez Pidal 13, tel: 963 49 72 22.
By boat
Estacío Marítima, El Grao. Trasmediterránea ferries to the Balearic Islands, tel: 902 45 46 45.

Alicante
By air
El Altet (12km/7 miles to the south); bus and taxis, tel: 965 26 84 00.

By rail
RENFE, Avenida de Salamanca, tel: 902 24 02 02. Madrid, Murcia, Barcelona. Estación de la Marina, tel: 965 26 27 31. There is a narrow-gauge line between Alicante and Dénia following a beautiful route close to the coast.
By bus
Calle Portugal, tel: 965 13 07 00. Nationwide connections.

Murcia
By air
San Javier (45km/28 miles to the east of Murcia), tel: 968 17 20 00.
By rail
Calle Industria (Barrio El Carmen), tel: 968 25 21 54.
By bus
Calle San Andrés, tel: 968 29 22 11.

Benidorm
By rail
Dénia/Alicante narrow-gauge railway, tel: 966 80 85 21.
By bus
Avenida Europa 8, tel: 966 80 39 55. València, Alicante, Guadalest, Alcoi and many other places.

Dénia
By rail
Alicante *(see above)*.

By bus
València, Alicante, Barcelona.
By boat
Ibiza (crossing: about 4 hours), Formentera, Mallorca (Línea Balearia, tel: 902 160 180; www.lineabalearia.com).

Facts for the Visitor

PASSPORTS AND VISAS
All non-Spanish visitors to the country require a passport or identity card. Visas are needed by all non-European Union nationals, unless their country has a reciprocal arrangement with Spain.

CUSTOMS
Citizens of non-EU member states can bring 400 cigarettes, one bottle of spirits, two of wine, 50g of perfume; citizens of EU-member states have guide levels of 800 cigarettes, 10 litres of spirit and 90 litres of wine. Customs keep a close watch for drugs, which are illegal.

TOURIST INFORMATION
The state-owned **Spanish National Tourist Office** will supply information to help plan your holiday. Here some addresses:

València Railway Station

OVERSEAS OFFICES

In the UK: 22–23 Manchester Square, London W1M 5AP, tel: 020 7486 8077, fax: 020 7486 8034, brochure line: 09063 640 630, email: info.londres@tourspain.es; www.tourspain.co.uk

In the US: 666 Fifth Avenue, New York, NY 10103, tel: 212 265 8822, fax: 212 265 8864, email: nuevayork@tourspain.es

INTERNET

Some other websites, with useful links and tourist information, you may wish to check out include: www.okspain.org, www.tourspain.es, www.comunitat-valenciana.es, www.red2000.com and www.turisvalencia.es

REGIONAL OFFICES IN SPAIN
València

Agència Valenciana del Turisme, Avenida Aragón 30, E-46021 València, tel: 963 98 60 00, fax: 963 98 00 01; www.comunidadvalenciana.com

Murcia

Dirección General de Turismo, San Cristóbal 6, E-30001 Murcia, tel: 968 35 86 00, fax: 968 36 61 10.

LOCAL OFFICES

Most towns have a local tourist office where English-speaking staff can provide town maps and other useful material. Here is a selection:

València

Calle de la Paz 48, tel: 963 98 64 22, fax: 963 98 64 21. Sub-offices at the airport and station.

Alicante

Rambla de Méndez Núñez 23, tel: 965 20 00 00, fax: 965 20 02 43.

Murcia

Plano de San Francisco, Palacio de Almudí, tel: 968 35 87 20, fax: 968 21 62 48.

Benidorm

Avenida Martínez Alejos 6, tel: 965 85 13 11, fax: 965 85 59 39.

Cartagena

Ayuntamiento, tel: 968 50 64 83, fax: 968 50 16 90.

Castelló

Plaza María Agustina 5, tel: 964 35 86 88, fax: 964 35 86 89.

Dénia

Plaza Oculista Buigues 9, tel: 966 42 23 67, fax: 965 78 09 57.

Peníscola

Paseo Marítimo, tel: 964 48 02 08, fax: 964 48 93 92.

Sagunt

Plaza Cronista Chabret, tel: 962 66 22 13, fax: 962 65 05 63.

CURRENCY AND EXCHANGE

In 2002, the euro (EUR) became the official currency used in Spain. Notes are denominated in 5, 10, 20, 50, 100 and 500 euros; coins in 1 and 2 euros and 1, 2, 5, 10, 20 and 50 cents.

The easiest way to obtain cash is with a credit/debit card and a PIN number at one of the many cash machines *(telebancos)*. Most shops and restaurants accept credit cards.

Spanish banks will change foreign currency and travellers' cheques, but charge a commission. Rates vary, so shop around. However, the Banco de España will change currency free of charge: in València: Calle Barcas 6; in Murcia: Calle Gran Vía 20; in Alicante: Rambla de Méndez Núñez 31.

TIPPING

Even for meals at all-in prices, a 5–10 percent *propina* is normal. In a bar or café it is usual to leave a few coins for the waiter. Hotel chambermaids usually expect a sum appropriate to your length of stay; porters 2 euros per item of luggage. When travelling by taxi, try to round up the fare.

OPENING TIMES

Shops: usually open 9.30am–1.30pm and 3.30–7/8pm; Saturday until 1pm. Food shops open a little earlier. Supermarkets often stay open all day until 10pm and are open on Sunday.

Banks: weekdays 9am–1.30pm, Saturday until noon. *Bureaux de change* have longer opening times, and some open on Saturday morning.

Museums: usually close Monday, Sunday afternoon and public holidays, plus weekdays 1–4pm. At some museums, citizens of EU countries can gain free entry by presenting their passport.

PUBLIC HOLIDAYS

National holidays: 1 January, 6 January (Epiphany), Good Friday, 1 May (Labour Day), Whitsuntide, 15 August (Assumption), 12 October (Christopher Columbus Day), 1 November (All Saints), 6 December (Constitution Day), 8 December (Immaculate Conception), 25 December.

In addition to national holidays, there are regional holidays for València cia and Murcia provinces, the dates of which vary from year to year. There are also various local holidays. During the *ferias* normal commercial life often comes to a standstill.

POST

Post offices *(correos)* are open weekdays 9am–2pm, 4–6pm and Saturday morning. Stamps *(sellos)* are available at tobacconists and some newsagents.

TELEPHONING

The easiest way to make a phone call is to go to a *Telefónica* office where you make your call and pay afterwards. It is possible to make international calls from all public telephones. Phone cards *(tarjeta telefónica)* for a range of values can be purchased at kiosks and tobacconists. Reduced tariffs for international calls apply 10pm–8am and all day Sunday.

To dial the UK from Spain, prefix your number with 00 44 and omit the first zero from the area code.

The country code for Spain is **34**.

All Spanish subscribers have nine-digit numbers. The first two or three digits are the provincial area code, e.g. Alicante and València: 96; Castelló 964; Murcia: 968.

General information: 10 03.

TIME

Spain is one hour ahead of Greenwich Mean Time (GMT plus 1). Summer time (GMT plus 2) is from late March until the last Sunday in September.

NEWSPAPERS

Newsagents keep a good supply of English newspapers, and periodicals, such as the weekly *Costa Blanca News,* are produced for English-speaking

---

Shopping and souvenirs

The province of València is famous for its pottery and ceramics. Attractive plates, jugs and glazed tiles are made in Agost, Onil and Biar. Lace scarves *(mantillas)*, linen and fans *(abanicos)* in the traditional style are available everywhere. Carpets and wall-hangings abound in Lorca and Crevillent. Basketware, made from reeds, esparto grass and palm leaves, is produced in Gata de Gorgos and Elx, inlaid work (chess boards, boxes) mainly in Murcia. Spanish designer fashion *(alta costura)* is very much in vogue, and shoes and leather accessories are relatively inexpensive.

If you want edible souvenirs to take home, choose from stuffed olives from the Alcoi, rice from Calasparra, *turrón* from Xixona, ham from Teruel or wine from Jumilla or Requena.

expatriates. These can be of interest as they contain advice about what's on and information about new restaurants.

VOLTAGE

This is usually 220V AC, but 110V in some rural areas. A continental adapter is essential for visitors from Britain.

DISABLED PEOPLE

The Spanish National Tourist Office (*see page 118*) publishes a fact sheet, listing a variety of useful addresses and some accessible accommodation.

Local tourist offices can advise on facilities and services in their area.

CLOTHING

You may feel a little conspicuous wearing brief shorts or bare-shoulder tops in the towns and larger centres. When visiting churches, wear discreet and respectable clothing. Most Spaniards like to dress up when going out in the evening.

MEDICAL ASSISTANCE

If an emergency arises, then you should go to the accident and emergency department of the nearest hospital, or summon help by dialling 091. If you have a less urgent medical need, then ask at your hotel or tourist office for the address of the nearest health centre (*centro de salud*) or the name of a recommended doctor, preferably English-speaking.

Although travellers from EU countries are advised to acquire the E111 certificate, which in theory entitles holders to use health facilities in any EU country free of charge, it is wise to have an accident and illness insurance policy. If you do need medical treatment, make sure you receive a detailed invoice (*factura*) to present to your insurance company.

A green cross on a white background is the symbol for a chemist (*farmácia*). Pharmacists are highly trained and can dispense many drugs that would be available only on prescription in many other countries. Emergency opening times are published in daily newspapers.

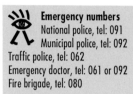

Emergency numbers
National police, tel: 091
Municipal police, tel: 092
Traffic police, tel: 062
Emergency doctor, tel: 061 or 092
Fire brigade, tel: 080

CRIME

To reduce the risk of car break-ins and theft, particularly in the main tourist centres and cities, always park your car in an attended car-park. Never leave anything of value in it and always keep the boot locked. Leave the glove compartment empty and visibly open. Larger quantities of money and valuable jewellery should be stored in the hotel safe.

Notify the police if you are the victim of theft, as your insurance company will need written confirmation when you submit your claim.

TIMESHARE TOUTS

Spanish property developers along the Costa Blanca often use aggressive methods to sell timeshare and apartments at 'preferential prices'. The property business is ridden with con men and shady characters. If you do wish to buy property or a share in property, take professional advice.

DIPLOMATIC REPRESENTATION

British Consulate: Plaza Calvo Sotelo 1-2, 03001 Alicante, tel: 965 21 61 90, fax: 965 14 05 28.

US Consulate General: Paseo Reina Elisenda de Montcada 23, 08034 Barcelona, tel: 93 280 2227.

ACCOMMODATION

There is no shortage of accommodation of all kinds in the Levant. On the contrary, apart from a few weeks during the high season, most hotels have rooms to spare. Many hotels in the main resorts close in winter. You are more likely to find quality accommodation typical of the region, away from the beaches, in the historic towns and rural villages. The Spanish National Tourist Office *(see page 118)* will supply a list of hotels categorised by region. Booking is advisable at Easter and from July to mid-September.

HOTELS

Hotels in Spain are categorised with stars, ranging from basic (∗) to luxury (∗∗∗∗∗). Prices range from 20 to 200 euros per double room. Not necessarily more basic than mid-range hotels, but usually smaller and more informal are **hostales**. These are categorised from ∗ to ∗∗∗. If the word **residencia** appears in the name, this means that food is not available. The most inexpensive forms of accommodation are **fonda** (a white F on a blue plate), **pensión** (P) and **casa de huespedes** (CH). Only in the luxury hotels and some holiday hotels do breakfast buffets come as standard. The official tariff (usually without breakfast) must be displayed in the lobby and in all rooms.

Paradores are state-run hotels set in favoured locations and usually occupying historic buildings, such as former monasteries or castles. However, the paradors in the Levant (Benicarló, El Saler, Xàbia, Puerta Lumbreras, Teruel) are all modern buildings. Central Reservation Office for Paradors in Spain: Calle Requena 3, 28013 Madrid, tel: 915 166 666; fax: 915 166 657; www.parador.es Agents in the UK are: Keytel International, 402 Edgware Road, London W2, tel: 020 7616 0300; fax: 020 7616 0317; email: paradors@keytel.co.uk

HOLIDAY FLATS AND APARTMENTS

Holiday flats and apartments are widely available and can usually be booked through travel agents. Try to avoid the *urbanizaciones*, sprawling holiday estates often with poor facilities; there are plenty of other, more attractive complexes to choose from.

Apartments and hotels,
Benidorm

YOUTH HOSTELS

Albergues juveniles are usually only open during July/August and prefer guests below the age of 26. For a directory of youth hostels in Spain, contact the Spanish National Tourist Office, or the National Youth Hostel Association, 8 St Stephen's Hill, St Albans, Herts AL1 2DY, tel: 01727 855215. Spanish *fondas* and the more basic *hostales* are in the same price range as youth hostels.

> **Campsites**
> There are campsites of all categories along the Mediterranean coast. Many also rent out holiday cabins *(cabañas)*. Not all sites are open all year. The Spanish National Tourist Office will supply a full list of campsites.

Hotel selection

The three main cities head the list; other place names follow in alphabetical order. €€€ means expensive, €€ medium priced and € inexpensive.

València

Excelsior, Barcelonina 5, tel: 963 51 46 12; www.hoteles-catalonia.es Recently renovated plush hotel in the centre. €€€.
Hospedería del Pilar, Mercado 19, tel: 963 91 66 00. Cheap but acceptable lodgings by the main market. €.
Jardín Botánico, 6 Doctor Peset Cervera, tel: 963 15 40 12; www.hotel jardinbotanico.com Charming new hotel, with spacious modern rooms. €€.
Meliá Confort Inglés, Marqués de Dos Aguas 6, tel: 963 51 64 26; www.solmelia.es In an elegant palace with attractive rooms and an excellent restaurant. €€.
Monte Picayo, Puzol, tel: 961 42 01 00; www.hvsl.es Luxury hotel, casino and a good restaurant, 20km (13 miles) from the city (exit 7 direction Barcelona on the A7). €€€.

Reina Victoria, Barcas 4, tel: 963 52 04 87; www.husa.es Classic city hotel, popular with *toreros*. €€€.
Venecia, En Llop 5, tel: 963 52 42 67, fax: 963 52 44 21. *Hostal* on the town hall square. Helpful staff. €€.

Alicante

Meliá, Playa del Postiguet, tel: 965 20 50 00; www.solmelia.es Good location between harbour and beach. €€€.
Les Monges, Las Monjas 2, tel: 965 21 50 46; www.lesmonges.net Lots of character in an 18th-century restored house. Go for the Japanese suite. €.
Hotel San Remo, Navas, tel: 965 20 95 00. Pleasant rooms on busy shopping street. €.
Sidi San Juan, Paraje Cabo de la Huerta, tel: 965 16 13 00; www.hoteles sidi.es Comfortable hotel by the beach (5km/3 miles). €€€.

Murcia

Arco de San Juan, Plaza Ceballos 10, tel: 968 21 04 55, fax: 968 22 08 09. Town hotel with style. €€€.
Hispano I, Trapería 8, tel: 968 21 61 52, fax: 968 21 68 59. Inexpensive hotel in the pedestrianised zone. €€.
Meliá Siete Coronas, Ronda de Garay 5, tel: 968 21 77 71; www.solmelia.es Functional and comfortably furnished. €€€.
Pensión Segura, Plaza de Camachas 14, tel: 968 21 12 81. Good value rooms with TV and bathroom. €.
Rincón de Pepe, Apóstoles 34, tel: 968 21 22 39; www.nh-hoteles.com Murcia's main rendez-vous since 1925. Stylishly modernised with a famous restaurant and smart night-club. €€€.

Aguilas

Madrid, Plaza Robles Vives 4, tel: 968 41 05 00. Reasonable value and good location. €.
El Paso, Cartagena 13, tel: 968 44 71 25, fax: 968 44 71 27. Inexpensive and comfortable; good restaurant. €.

Alcoi

Mas de Pau, Carretera Alcoi-Penáguila, 9km (6 miles), tel: 965 51 31 58. Nicely renovated farmhouse in the heart of the Sierra. €€.

Reconquista, Pont de Sant Jordi 1, tel: 965 33 09 00; www.hotelodon.com Neat, tidy and central town hotel with a sister hotel 'Odon' around the corner. €€.

Altea

Cap Negret, Carretera València-Alicante, 159km (98 miles), tel: 965 84 12 00; www.hotelcapnegret.com Modern hotel by the beach. €€€.

Hostal Fornet, Beniardá 1, tel: 965 84 30 05. Clean comfortable rooms in the heart of the old town. €.

Campsite: **Cap Blanch**, Playa del Albir, tel: 965 84 59 46.

Ares del Maestre

D'Ares, Plaza Mayor 4, Ares del Maestre, tel: 964 44 30 07, fax: 964 44 32 34. Restored farmhouse, 12 rooms, personal service and good food. €€.

Benicarló

Marynton, Paseo Marítimo 5, tel: 964 47 30 11, fax: 964 46 07 20. Unpretentious urban hotel close to harbour; also apartments. €€.

Parador Costa de Azahar, Avenida Papa Luna 3, tel: 964 47 01 00; www.parador.es Modern, concrete building in a good location by the sea. €€€.

Benidorm

Bilbaíno, Avenida Virgen del Sufragio 1, tel: 965 85 08 04. Good value friendly hotel on the beachfront. €€.

Gran Hotel Delfín, Avenida Mont Benidorm 13, tel: 965 85 34 00; www.webic.com/granhoteldelfin Quietly situated hotel with Castilian-style dark furniture overlooking the beach. €€.

Jaime 1, Avenida Jaime I 9, tel/fax: 965 85 07 44. Recently refurbished comfortable hotel. €€.

Les Dunes Comodoro, Avenida Madrid, Playa Levante, tel: 966 80 32 16; www.lesdunes.com 23-storey apartment block with swimming pool, on the promenade. €€.

Selomar, Virgen del Sufragio, tel: 965 85 52 77, fax: 965 85 44 14. Near the old town and right by the sea. €€€.

Campsite: **Villasol**, Avenida de l'Admiral Bernat de Sarria, tel: 965 85 04 22. Smart site in the top category.

Calp

Galetamar, La Caleta 28-A, tel: 965 83 23 11; www.galetamar.com Six-storey building, near the beach. €€€.

Roca Esmeralda, Ponent 1, tel: 965 83 61 01; www.unytursa.com Modern hotel; swimming pool and disco. €€.

Venta la Chata, Carretera N-332, 149km (92 miles), tel/fax: 965 83 03 08. Former post-house with rustic atmosphere, sea views and tennis courts. €€.

Campsite: **Ifach**, Carretera Calpe-Moraira, 5km (3 miles), tel: 965 83 04 77.

Caravaca de la Cruz

Central, Gran Vía 18, tel: 968 70 70 55, fax: 968 70 73 69. Convenient and comfortable with spacious modern rooms. €€.

Cartagena

Cartagonova, Marcos Redondo 3, tel: 968 50 42 00; www.hotelcartagonova.com Pleasant central, recently renovated hotel with a fresh new look. €€€.

Los Habaneros, San Diego 60, tel: 968 50 52 50; www.hotelhabaneros.com Large modern hotel with excellent facilities. €€.

Peninsular, Cuatro Santos 3, tel: 968 50 00 33. Modest, old-town hotel. €.

Castelló

Intur Castelló, Herrero 20, tel: 964 22 50 00; www.intur.com Modern, central and comfortable. €€€.

NH Mindoro, Moyano 4, tel: 964 22 23 00; www.nh-hoteles.com Older town hotel in a good position. €€.

Cullera
Carabela II, Avenida Diagonal del País Valencià 41, tel: 961 72 40 70. Central, modern hotel, in-house cafeteria. €€.
Santa Marta, Playa del Racó, tel: 961 73 80 29, fax: 961 73 29 95. A modern hotel situated right by the beach. €€.
Campsite: **Santa Marta**, Carretera al Faro, tel: 961 72 14 40.

Dénia
Costa Blanca, Pintor Llorens 3, tel: 965 78 03 36; www.hotelcostablanca.com A pleasant comfortable hotel near the train station. €€.
La Racona, Carretera Les Rotes 76, tel: 965 78 79 60; www.hotel-laracona.com Small beach hotel with swimming pool and garden; apartments also available. €€.
Rosa, Congre, La Marina, tel: 965 78 15 73, fax: 966 42 47 74. Attractive complex near the beach. €€.

El Saler
Luis Vives, Carretera Saler (16km/10 miles), tel: 961 61 11 86; www.parador.es Modern parador between the beach and lagoon, with a famous golf-course. €€€.
Sidi Saler, Playa del Saler, tel: 961 61 04 11; www.hotelessidi.es Comfortable hotel which has benefitted from recent renovation. €€€.

Elx
Candilejas, Dr. Ferrán 19, tel: 965 46 65 12. Functional *hostal*. €.
Huerto del Cura, Porta de la Morera 14, tel: 966 61 00 11; www.huertodelcura .com Among the palm trees. Comfortable. €€€.

Forcall
Palau dels Osset, Plaza Mayor 16, tel: 964 17 75 24; www.hotelpalau.com Four-star hotel, suitable for disabled people, with 20 rooms. €€.

Gandia
Bayren I, Passeig Marítim Neptú 62, tel: 962 84 03 00; www.hotelesbayren.com By the sea. Dancing with live orchestra during the season. €€€.
Borgia, Avenida República Argentina 5, tel: 962 87 81 09; www.hghoteles.com Modern and comfortable. In the town centre. €€.
Los Robles, Formentera 33, tel: 962 84 21 00, fax: 962 84 15 49. 100m (110yds) from the beach; nice swimming pool, large garden. €€.
Hotel La Safor, Carretera de València 40, tel: 962 86 40 11. In the centre of town with parking and buffet breakfast. €.
Campsite: **L'Alquería**, Carretera Gandia-Playa de Gandia (2km/1.2 miles), tel: 962 84 04 70; www.lalqueria.com

Guardamar del Segura
Hotel Meridional with **El Jardín** restaurant, Avenida de la Libertad 64, tel: 965 72 83 40; www.hotelmeridional.es A rarity on the Costa Blanca: a hotel near the beach with a special atmosphere and good, local cooking. €€.

Igluesuela del Cid
Casa Amada, Fuente Nueva 10, tel: 964 44 33 73. Clean and friendly. €.

La Manga del Mar Menor
Doblemar, Gran Vía, tel: 968 56 39 10, fax: 968 14 09 98. Comfortable hotel block with casino. €€.
Dos Mares, Plaza Bohemia, tel: 968 14 00 93, fax: 968 14 03 22. Central, convenient and reasonably priced. €€.
Hyatt Regency La Manga, Los Belones, tel: 968 33 12 34; www.lamanga. hyatt.com A 450-hectare (1,100-acre) luxury village with grand hotel, apartments and 18-hole golf course. €€€.
Villas La Manga, Gran Vía, tel: 968

14 52 22; www.villaslamanga.es Of almost family proportions, beside the Mar Menor. €€.

La Vila Joiosa

El Montíboli, Partida Montíboli, tel: 965 89 02 50; www.relaischateaux.com/montiboli Built on a rock in Moorish style; two swimming pools, sheltered beach: one of the finest hotels on the Costa Blanca. €€€.

Los Alcázares

La Encarnación, Condesa 1, tel: 968 57 50 07. 1904 Spa hotel with lots of character and good facilities. €€.

Lorca

Amaltea, La Torrecilla, Carretera de Granada, tel: 968 40 65 65; www.nh-hoteles.com Modern and comfortable, but a fair way from the centre. €€€.

Los Urrutias

Estrella del Mar, tel: 968 13 43 00, fax: 968 13 43 63. Relatively discreet *urbanización*. Apartments. €€.

Moratalla

Cenajo, Pantano del Cenajo, tel: 968 72 10 11, fax: 968 72 06 45. Situated 28km (17 miles) to the north of the town, occupying a former engineer's house by the reservoir. Isolated but pretty. Restaurant. €€.

Morella

Cardenal Ram, Cuesta Suñer 1, tel: 964 17 30 85, fax: 964 17 32 18. Romantic hotel in a 16th-century palace with just 19 rooms. €€.
El Cid, Puerta de San Mateo 3, tel: 964 16 01 25. Spick and span small hotel with wonderful views. €.
Fábrica de Giner, Carretera Zorita, 4.5km (2 miles), tel: 964 17 31 42, fax: 964 17 31 97. Converted weaving mill below the town. Comfortable spot and an ideal starting point for walking

enthusiasts. €€.
Rey Don Jaime, Juan Giner 6, tel: 964 16 09 11; www.reydonjaimemorella.com Friendly and comfortable. €€.

Oliva

Campsites: **Bon Día**, tel: 962 85 15 63; **Euro Cámping**, tel: 962 85 40 98. Campsite: **Los Llanos**, Carretera N-322, 203km (125 miles), tel: 965 75 51 88.

Orihuela

Rey Teodomiro, Avenida Teodomiro 10, tel: 966 74 33 48. Centrally-located *hostal*. €.

Orpesa del Mar

Marina, Paseo Marítimo 12, tel/fax: 964 31 00 99. Smart modern hotel in a good location. Full pensión only in height of summer. €€€.
Neptuno Playa, Paseo Marítimo 1, tel: 964 31 00 40, fax: 964 31 00 75. Mid-range hotel by the sea. €€.

Peníscola

Los Delfines, Avenida Papa Luna 4, tel: 964 48 13 61; www.hotellosdelfines.com Modern hotel, with restaurant on terrace and live music in summer. €€.
Del Duc, Fuladosa 10, tel: 964 48 07 68. Informal pension in the historic town centre. €.

Holidays in the country
Away from the beaches, up in the starkly beautiful Maestrazgo region and in Murcia's northeast, many old farmhouses *(casas rurales)* have been renovated and are now rented to holidaymakers.

The main companies to contact are: Turistrat (Plaça Gaspar Fuster 13, 12140 Albocasser, tel: 964 42 84 32, fax: 964 42 83 58) and Asociación de Alojamientos Rurales de la Montaña Alicantina (Masía del Pinet, 03459 Alfafara, tel/fax: 965 52 90 39; www.cederaitana.com).

Hostería del Mar, Avenida Papa Luna 18, tel: 964 48 06 00; www.hosteria delmar.net Upmarket beach hotel. Medieval banquet on Saturdays. Rustic furnishing. €€€.

Hotel-Restaurante Simo, Porteta 5, tel: 964 48 06 20. Small hotel with excellent restaurant in the centre of old town with sea views. €€.

Puerto de Mazarrón
Bahía, Playa de la Reya, tel: 968 59 40 00. Modern hotel by the beach. €€.

Sagunt
Azahar, Avenida País València 8, tel: 962 66 33 68, fax: 962 65 01 75. Small, respectable hotel in town centre. €€.

El Bergantín, Plaza del Sol 6 (Puerto de Sagunt), tel: 962 68 03 59; www. elbergantin.com Simple, clean and friendly, and close to the beach. €.

San Pedro del Pinatar
Neptuno, Avenida Generalísimo 6, tel: 968 18 19 11; www.hotelneptuno.net Modern hotel in a central location. Friendly. €€.

Santa Pola
Marina Palace, Carretera Alicante–Cartagena Km17, tel: 965 41 13 12; www.hotelmarinapalace.com Luxurious hotel with all the usual facilities including tennis court, gym and pool. €€€.

Patilla, Elx 29, tel: 965 41 10 15; www.hotelpatilla.com Basic hotel in a central location. €€.

Polamar, Astilleros 12, tel: 965 41 32 00; www.polamar.com Right by Playa de Levante. Neat and tidy. €€.

Campsite: **Bahía de Santa Pola**, N-332, tel: 965 41 10 12, fax: 965 41 67 90. Campsite open year round.

Teruel
Civera, Avenida Sagunto 37, tel/fax: 978 60 23 00. Respectable mid-range hotel. €€.

Oriente, Avenida Sagunto 5, tel: 978 60 15 50, fax: 978 60 10 64. Simple, neat and tidy. €€.

Parador de Teruel, Carretera Zaragoza, tel: 978 60 18 00; www.parador.es Modern hotel located just outside the town. €€€.

Reina Cristina, Ovalo 1, tel: 978 60 68 60; www.gargallo-hotels.com Ideally located on the edge of the old town. Friendly and comfortable. €€€.

Vinaròs
Duc de Vendôme, Carretera N-340, 144.4km (89 miles), tel: 964 45 09 44. Inexpensive hotel outside town. €€.

Miramar, Blasco Ibáñez 12, tel/fax: 964 45 14 00. Pleasant old-fashioned hotel by the beach promenade. €€.

Xàbia
Parador de Xàbia, Avenida del Mediterráneo 7, tel: 965 79 02 00; www. parador.es Modern complex by the sea. Lovely gardens. €€€.

Villa Mediterránea, León 5, Carretera Xàbia-Jesús Pobre, tel: 965 79 52 33; www.hotelvillamed.com Top-class hotel (7 rooms) in a great location. €€€.

Miramar, Almirante Bastarreche 12, tel: 965 79 01 00. Central location overlooking the harbour. Good value, friendly atmosphere. €€.

Xàtiva
Hostería Montsant, Carretera del Castillo, tel: 962 27 50 81, fax: 962 28 19 05. A real gem. Seven tastefully furnished rooms, and a huge orange grove. Ideal location between town and fortress. €€€.

Murta, Angel Lacalle 3, tel: 962 27 66 11, fax: 962 27 65 50. Pleasant, comfortable hotel near the city centre. 21 large rooms and a good restaurant offering a variety of specialities. €€.

Vernissa, Académico Maravall 1, tel: 962 27 10 11, fax: 962 28 13 65. Central, town hotel. €€.

☄ INSIGHT COMPACT GUIDES

Great Little Guides to the following destinations:

Algarve
Amsterdam
Antigua/Barbuda
Athens
Bahamas
Bali
Bangkok
Barbados
Barcelona
Beijing
Belgium
Berlin
Bermuda
Brittany
Bruges
Brussels
Budapest
Burgundy
California
Cambodia
Cancún & the
   Yucatán
Chile
Copenhagen
Costa Brava
Costa del Sol
Costa Rica
Crete
Cuba
Cyprus
Czech Republic
Denmark
Dominican
Republic
Dublin
Egypt

Finland
Florence
French Riviera
Goa
Gran Canaria
Greece
Holland
Hong Kong
Ibiza
Iceland
Ireland
Israel
Italian Lakes
Italian Riviera
Jamaica
Jerusalem
Kenya
Laos
Lisbon
Madeira
Madrid
Mallorca
Malta
Menorca
Milan
Montreal
Morocco
Moscow
Munich
Normandy
Norway
Paris
Poland
Portugal
Prague
Provence

Rhodes
Rio de Janeiro
Rome
St. Lucia
St. Petersburg
Salzburg
Shanghai
Singapore
Southern Spain
Sri Lanka
Switzerland
Sydney
Tahiti
Tenerife
Thailand
Toronto
Turkey
Turkish Coast
Tuscany
Venice
Vienna
Vietnam
West of Ireland

UK regional:
Bath &
   Surroundings
Belfast
Cambridge &
   East Anglia
Cornwall
Cotswolds
Devon & Exmoor
Edinburgh
Glasgow
Guernsey

Jersey
Lake District
London
New Forest
North York Moors
Northumbria
Oxford
Peak District
Scotland
Scottish
Highlands
Shakespeare
   Country
Snowdonia
South Downs
York
Yorkshire Dales

USA regional:
Boston
Cape Cod
Chicago
Florida
Florida Keys
Hawaii – Maui
Hawaii – Oahu
Las Vegas
Los Angeles
Martha's Vineyard
   & Nantucket
Miami
New Orleans
New York
San Diego
San Francisco
Washington DC

Insight's checklist to meet all your travel needs:

■ *Insight Guides* provide the complete picture, with expert cultural background and stunning photography. Great for travel planning, for use on the spot, and as a souvenir. 186 titles.

■ *Insight Museums & Galleries* guides to London, Paris, Florence and New York provide comprehensive coverage of each city's cultural temples and lesser known collections.

■ *Insight Pocket Guides* focus on the best choices for places to see and things to do, picked by our correspondents. They include large fold-out maps. More than 130 titles.

■ *Insight Compact Guides* are the fact-packed books to carry with you for easy reference when you're on the move in a destination. More than 130 titles.

■ *Insight FlexiMaps* combine clear, detailed cartography with essential information and a laminated finish that makes the maps durable and easy to fold. 133 titles.

The world's largest collection of visual travel guides and maps

INDEX